Deathbed Reflections

by

One of Many

Deathbed Reflections

Copyright © 2020 by Ward Joseph Jarman

All rights reserved. No part of this book may be reproduced or transmitted in any form or by any means without written permission of the author.

ISBN 978-1-943424-59-7

Library of Congress Control Number: 2019953631

North Country Press
Unity, Maine

We are:
the consequences of the past;
the foundations of the future.

Preface

I do not know the year in which Mark Twain wrote *The War Prayer*. I was given an illustrated copy of it by a good college friend in 1969 or 1970. The illustrations were all done in brown (rust brown on the red side and more transparent than opaque). Second only to the message contained in *The War Prayer* is the fact that it was published only after Mark Twain had died. It was his wish that it not be published until after he had been placed in Earth and covered with dirt. On the back cover of my copy is a quote by Mark Twain indicating his reason for not allowing publication until after his death. What I remember of this quote is: "I have told the whole truth and only dead men can tell the truth..."

It is with this sentiment that I pen my deathbed reflections. I do not seek to prove any point presented in this reflection. Dead men (or women) don't need to prove anything. This reflection is about what I have learned, correctly or incorrectly.

Table of Contents

Autobiographical Sketch 1

The Need to be Educated 35

Consequences and Foundations 59

The 'Holy-men' of the Roman Catholic Church (RCC) are Hiding Behind Their 'God' 67

How the Individual is Critical 77

To Educate...or...to Train 89

We, the People; Institutional Pillars of the Community, and Corruption 99

Sex, Food and Humanity 125

The Function of Us 139

To Summarize What I Have Learned (Correctly or Incorrectly) 149

About the Author 163

Autobiographical Sketch

I am dying. But I am not dying like all humans who travel to death from the time of their birth. I am caught in a diagnosed terminal illness. My nemesis is a rare cancer of the blood. If it goes sideways and morphs into a virulent form of leukemia, I will have six weeks or so to live. Otherwise, I am left to simply struggle with the challenges of managing the symptoms of the progressive diminishing of my body's various systems. Each new slight pain, each aggravating disfunction no matter how slight is a constant reminder that my physical body is breaking down. Each reminder whispers the reality of my mortality, not in a cognitive, intellectual sense, but in a flesh and blood, in your face, fact -- "You're dying. This is your reality. You're leaving Earth." While this doesn't happen every day, it does happen weekly at least. An ache in my spleen is more constant than an occasional intermittent occurrence. Death, my real death is on my mind.

How does one cope with facing the pitch black, all-encompassing void of the absolute unknowable? Having looked deep into the place where no light exists, I have chosen to turn around, placing my back to the void, and face the path of my life's journey. To my thinking, it is quite possible that one dies the same way one lived. This is a reality not easily perceived until one truly faces the empty blackness of one's personal death. When a person is left to encounter, face to face, the true absence of everything knowable (including the absence of light) or face the truth of one's own life, that individual will face the opposing fear of his or her existence. What do I fear more, facing the reality of the void or facing the reality of the truth of my life? The reader of these pages does not have to take me at my word for this. I do not care. For me, at this place in my life, I am certain all readers of my words will, at some point in their journey, face the truth or untruth of my stated position.

As I am seated upon my death bed, there is no need for lies, no need for defenses. I am leaving. If I am to be judged it will be by an authority that cannot be deceived, hood-winked or distracted. My reputation on Earth is of no consequence to me. I will not be here to endure the outrage, nor will I be able to enjoy any pleasantries bestowed upon me. I am free to speak my mind as I will. Take it or leave it. It is all the same to me.

This nakedness, the raw truth of my life's activities and the true motivations behind those actions can be covered over by any one of the many organized 'religious faiths' that are available throughout the human community. These have various means for forgiving transgressions and punishments promised for the unrepentant, a whole array of customs and procedures to dampen the unadulterated sting of the accuracy of your soul's naked true self. This, my friend, is the ultimate face of true judgment, the stripping away of all rationalizations, defenses, self-deceptions, avoidances, and all other mannerisms of human attempts to minimize any and all harsh truths manifesting themselves before our trembling, naked selves -- authentic, genuine, crystal clear, pristine self-judgment. If one believes in the basic goodness of all life and tries to the best of their abilities to nurture that goodness, then one need not fear. Such an individual will survive such a reckoning.

This observation is not meant to take away from any and all beneficial practices that function to nurture the goodness of all life known to humans as pronounced and performed throughout those organized religions. Any and all things that nurture the goodness of all life are commendable, self-rewarding and consistent with the evolving Universe. What I am alluding is that membership in any of the professed religious organizations within the human community (this includes atheists and agnostics) does not pardon any individual from the above, final accounting of one's life upon this planet. It is my belief that each and every individual must come to understand the naked truth of his or her life regardless of any desire (or lack thereof) to know that truth. This is the tough love of a beneficial judgment, not for the sentencing of punitive pain, but for the purpose of enlightening the individual facing the day of reckoning. Whatever pain is experienced is not inflicted by any outside force and is not the focus of the required experience; but, if present, is the natural consequence of the event. That being the case, why should I approach such an experience unpracticed, unprepared and untrained. So it is that I write these words. However, I, being the frail and flawed human that I am, shall begin gradually and see where I end up.

I am now a Type II diabetic. As stated previously, I have been diagnosed with a rare blood disorder that cannot be cured. I produce too many red blood cells which "muddies up" my blood making me a good candidate for heart attacks and strokes. Additionally, the red blood cells are not formed properly and do not carry oxygen efficiently -- so I'm told. My only treatment is to drain a pint of blood if my blood count is higher than the designated level for treatment. If the blood count is higher, then I bleed a pint. If not, then I have a reprieve until we check the blood count again in four weeks. When I was first diagnosed with this problem I had to bleed a pint of blood every week for sixteen weeks before my blood count finally got below the targeted acceptable blood count. Some individuals might be able to go three months between bleeds. But, if I'm too unfortunate and become a rare individual whose white blood cell count jumps up to plummet me into a vicious form of leukemia, then I would have about six weeks to live, so I've been told. The shock on my face and my tear-filled eyes caused my doctor to assure me, "But that is a rare occurrence." My response, "But this is a rare disease so I'm good with rare."

The shock of this diagnosis was like the shock of diving into a cold pool of clear water on a very, very hot day in summer when the sun is high in a clear windless sky. Such cold truth takes your breath away. It was this shock that placed me under the freshly laundered, cold linens of my death bed on a bitterly cold winter's night. It was this shock that greeted me the next morning after my body had heated my deathbed into a toasty warm little oven. My cool face and cold nose alerted me to the fact that I had to rise out of bed and confront the cold air of my wintery house to get dressed in the cold and face the winter's day.

Today, November 2, 2018, I am getting acclimated to the passing of summer and the ending of fall to survive the Maine winter and all of its nuances, pleasantries and challenges (the shoveling of snow, possible power outages, and keeping the house warm).

At the present time, the world abounds with experts. Professional information pushers known as spin doctors, lobbyists, public relations personnel and/or publicists present 'expert' after 'expert' to explain the "truthfulness" of the presented point of view. Any statement made that does not flow from the mouth of an expert must be suspect, naive, inaccurate and/or grossly oversimplified. The voice of the average citizen attempting to live a life as best as circumstances allow is without value. It is without value because it is perceived as a life without power. It is without power because extremely wealthy individuals, huge national and multinational corporations, and too big to fail banks have the fast sums of money to move society in the direction consistent with their perception of the way it should be. The services of professional information pushers must be purchased with sizable paychecks. The average worker living paycheck to paycheck cannot afford such professional information pushers to present their perspectives. Thus, reality, it appears, is what power dictates. That being the case, I present my credentials upon which I speak.

First of all, and of the highest importance, is that I am seated upon my death bed. As I have stated, I have no need to lie; I do not seek to persuade or prove anything. I am simply making an accounting of what I believe I have learned correctly or incorrectly. I have no need for defenses. In the end I will be defenseless against my required self-judgment based upon the raw truth of my life's activities and the true motivations behind those actions. I am leaving.

My other credentials are as follows:

I have been divorced. I am in my second marriage. The divorce process was extremely painful, and I swore that I would never marry again. So much for my sacred oaths, a topic I must take up later. I have twin sons who are now solidly in adulthood. One twin has served in the army and has earned his master's degree. The other twin has been a special needs individual from birth. He was a slow-to-thrive, soft tonal baby that had great difficulty feeding. The twin who earned his master's degree was five pounds, thirteen ounces at birth while his brother was four pounds, fourteen ounces. Both were premature. It is clear to me that we are all not born equal. As for my own birth order, I am the youngest of three boys.

My mother was a devout Roman Catholic and steadfastly raised her family to be devout Catholics. The whole family attended Mass every Sunday. Dad was absent when he worked overtime or had to sleep due to working a double shift at the plant. All major religious holidays or events were duly observed with whatever the Church's dictates prescribed. My mother made certain that my brothers and I attended the local Catholic grammar school. It was her obligation to make sure that all of her sons received a Roman Catholic education. To this end, she sent my eldest brother away to a Catholic high school. I and my other brother were spared such a fate. My mother was a homemaker until I entered the ninth grade. At that time she gained employment at a local men's clothing store.

My father was a hard-working man, but getting a job (a good job) did not happen so easily. He met my mother during the war after he was drafted into the army and stationed abroad. He married her after he was discharged from the armed services. Before he married her, he underwent the procedure to convert to the Roman Catholic Church and be baptized in my mother's faith. Such was the power of the Church in my mother's life. A year or so after being discharged, he, his new wife and their first-born son returned to the United States. He wanted to be a state policeman and applied, but was rejected because his physical build did not meet the regulations. Being the third born of three sons, I do not remember too much of the early years of my parents' growing family. I do remember that there were times, during my younger years, that we didn't always have enough to eat. I remember my dad fixing a bowl of cocoa for me and breaking up a few pieces of white bread to float in the cocoa. He told me that this was a special treat for me for dinner since Mom wasn't home. I was very young and I believed him. As I grew older, I came to understand that there were some rough times for my family. When Mom started working after I finished grammar school, Dad was working diligently to improve his employment and paycheck in his attempt to become an electrician.

My father's father was a tenant farmer who sired thirteen children. So my father grew up in a large farming family in which everyone had to contribute to the work at hand. This is probably the fertile ground from which my father's work ethic flourished. After several different job attempts, my father finally gained employment in a factory about an hour's drive from home. He was employed in that factory until his retirement.

His first job at the plant was that of a regular lineman under the supervision of a foreman. I remember several times while growing up that a kind of fear or at least some kind of deep concern seeped into our household. When I became older, I came to understand this apprehension was stimulated by the plant laying off scores of individuals because the plant did not have enough orders to operate at full or near full capacity. Layoffs were according to seniority. The fate of my father's employment depended upon my father's position on the seniority list and how many individuals had to be let go. We never knew how deep each of the layoffs would be, so we just had to wait until the layoffs ended. We watched as the layoff line rose toward Dad's date of hire.

I am sure that my dad was quite anxious during those times. To improve his job security, Dad jumped at the chance to apply for a trainee position to become an electrician to work on the machines at the plant. Members of the electrician's shop were never part of the layoff procedure. He had to take a test to see if he had the mathematical and mechanical aptitude required to complete course work at an accredited trade school. He passed the test and carpooled with several other coworkers in our area to attend night school after work. After he became a working member of the electrician's shop, he not only improved his job security but also had an opportunity to accrue many overtime hours which he rarely turned down. He was able to retire four years early based on his overtime work record.

My mother and father both finished high school but never attended college. Being bound and determined that all three of her sons would graduate from college and being a devout Catholic, my mother scraped enough money together to send all three of her sons to the private school (Catholic of course) that was supported by our local parish. The teaching staff was mostly nuns but there were a few priests and one or two lay employees who took a role in teaching from time to time. My performance during my grammar school years did not hold much promise for becoming a college graduate. My older brothers on the other hand held great promise. Each was granted admission to advanced Latin classes (wishful thinking for developing an early desire to pursue a vocation in the clergy) and mathematics classes during their later years (seven and eighth grades) while I was relegated to the classes for the less academically inclined students.

Each and every student had to take the annual class in religious instruction to learn how to be a good Roman Catholic. All of the teachings of the Catholic Church, everything about each of the sacraments; a complete and in depth understanding of the Holy Mass; how to correctly complete the Stations of the Cross; the Corporal and Spiritual Works of Mercy, and all of the required prayers had to be learned and learned well. Everything about being a devout Roman Catholic had to be completely understood (and practiced, at least at school,) whether or not you were baptized as a Catholic and regardless of your academic prowess. Every Friday each grade would be escorted to the church where all of the Catholic students who had received their First Communion went to confession in preparation for Mass the following Sunday. Non-Catholics sat in the pews with the rest of the grade and had to wait patiently until all of that grade's confessions were heard; then back to school we all went. I though it strange that non-Catholics would send their children to a Catholic school especially with the mandated requirement of learning all about the Roman Catholic religion, but I later learned that this grammar school had an excellent educational reputation.

The math classes I attended were more of the garden variety kind and while everyone took a class in literature, I was enrolled in an additional class in English composition to offset the Latin classes granted to the more substantial students. Additionally, I was slow in learning to read. To this day I read slowly. During my years at this school, I developed the belief that I was a poor student because I was lacking in intelligence and/or work ethic to achieve at my brothers' level of performance. This was reinforced in my latter years when I was introduced frequently to a newly hired nun as Bernard and Bradley's little brother. This was an innocent enough introduction except for the knowingly exchanged looks between the nuns. I had established a reputation for myself. The looks indicated that it was not a highly sought after reputation. Upon graduating from grammar school and transitioning into a public high school, some nun of authority held a conference with my mother. I was present and the one part of this conference that I remember to this day was that nun telling my mother, "I think you should enroll him in a vocational training school instead of the college preparation program. I don't believe that he will even see the shadow of a college much less be admitted into one."

This was not to my mother's liking. She ignored the sincerely, nonjudgmental advice offered as an attempt to help all parties to experience a good and fruitful life. As I have said, my mother's determination to have all of her sons be very well educated (and graduate from college) was extremely unyielding. I was enrolled in and took the college preparatory high school classes. My brothers still out-performed me in all things academic and nonacademic. I was the average student within the collective group of average students, or so I thought.

As it turned out, when I looked at my high school record years later, I was a good student with some scores above average in mathematics and science while my scores in English were average or below. What I have discovered as an adult is that my visual impairment had handicapped me but there were no offsetting educational adaptations presented to me. It wasn't the way Catholic schools operated back then, nor were public schools so versed in special education issues. The birth defect that impacted my vision rendered my right eye pretty much dysfunctional visually. When my left eye is open, the right eye pretty much shuts down. Visually, my brain prevents the right eye from forming any image (so I have been told) by ever so slightly oscillating back and forth. Preventing the right eye from forming an image prevents me from seeing a double image. Well into my adult years, I researched if anything could be done to help overcome this handicapping situation. I was advised that I could go through an intense visual training process but in the end there would be no guarantee that I would work through the phase of seeing a double image. "You mean I would be stuck in the situation of always seeing a double image?" There was no guarantee that would not happen. I decided to keep what I had. I had survived this far in my life with this handicap. I did not want the challenge of developing new strategies to overcome the handicap of seeing double images all of the time.

Being somewhat of a Cyclops impacts the reading process significantly. In simple terms, my visual field is predominately the visual field of my left eye. Thus when reading I track across the page slowly and, often times, I drop down, skipping the next line on the page (become confused) and must re-track to the proper next line. Thus the slow reading behavior. All of my reading tests were timed tests. I never finished any one reading test and all questions not answered were counted as incorrect answers. Thusly, my reading scores were always low. However, the questions that I did answer were correct to a very high degree.

The well-meaning nun's prediction before my mother and myself was proven incorrect. I did gain access to a college and earned a B.A. degree in English Studies, after which I earned a Master of Education degree.

After completing my formal education, I embarked upon establishing a career path. There was, however, a significant speed bump (or two or three) across my career path as a professional educator. This (or these) speed bumps were of my own creation. While I obtained my mother's great desire to become well educated, I may not have achieved good common sense regarding the marketplace environment.

You may have surmised that gaining my degrees was more difficult for me than the average college student due to my visual handicap especially after my decision to major in English studies which would require a large amount of reading. If this is not what you have surmised, I will be more direct. The reading required for my B.A. in English Studies was very taxing. I spent more time reading than my fellow English majors, not because I was reading more, but because I was reading more slowly. Needless to say, by the time I was almost finished with my master's degree course work, I ached for a change of venue. I had one course to complete for my master's and one semester of student teaching to accomplish before I could receive my teaching certificate. I completed the course work, so I would receive my master's degree, but I balked at the student teaching part.

As an undergraduate student I had a professor who was my favorite and a most difficult faculty member in the English department. I took as many courses from him as I could schedule. He, being a professor of English literature and language, loved to play around with words. He may have wrecked me. The jury is still out on this issue because I have yet to live my full life though I am nearing its final ending point.

During my first class with him, he delivered a lecture that instantly set or defined my compass reading for the trajectory of my educational beam:

"Information, to be informed, is to be changed," I heard. It instantly made sense to me. To be informed means that one's form was to be altered. Once informed, that which is taken "in" should affect and/or effect your "form". Outstanding!

"Enthusiasm, 'en theos', in the spirit. You should be enthusiastic about what you learn," is also what I heard as he wrote on the board. "To be in the spirit of the information at hand and feel its affect and effect; and to be opened to a modification of your form (your life)," he added.

"What you need here, in this place, is a muse." The function of education, the function of being educated, is to change your form, your life (hopefully for the better).

"This is not a trade school. Your purpose here is not about developing a trade. Education, education here, is about enlightenment; to be in the spirit for the purpose of being altered, changed (hopefully for the better)," may not be what he said. Even if he did not say these words, these are the words I heard.

Native American spirituality has spirits that come in a good way and others that are tricksters and some that are bad spirits. So when meeting a muse one must be careful. One must be careful about what information is taken in and watchful about how that information resonates; how it corresponds with previous information encountered; its internal consistencies and inconsistencies, and how it rings true or false. While being opened to being informed, one must be cautious about being misinformed. Knowing the difference is a critical aspect of being educated. Outstanding! I was sold. I was not in college for grades. I was here for the process of becoming informed which would change my form, my way of living.

So, when I finally had to register for my semester of student teaching, I may have over-thought the situation. Perhaps I became seduced by a trickster spirit, or perhaps there was a part of me not yet properly educated and some spirit of the universe needed to inform me of some important aspect of reality. Whatever was the case, this is how I reasoned out my situation back then.

I would have to pay tuition for the semester to student teach. Additionally, I would have to pay a student teaching fee on top of the regular tuition. For this expenditure I would have the privilege of doing all of the work of teaching for my supervising teacher who would actually not do much of any of the planning or teaching of the classes for which he or she would be paid their normal salary. Right? This situation, I surmised, was indentured servitude if not a form of modernized slavery. If I was to do all of the work and would be required to pay for the privilege, then the teacher would be paid to do very little or nothing at all if I was exemplary in my student teaching. This is the point in my thinking where the professor's lecture about being informed, being enlightened, being in the spirit, and living what you learn descended upon me to challenge me to stay true to what I believed was the reality that I should live. Slavery, indentured servitude, and all forms of exploitation were wrong and should not be reinforced and encouraged, much less supported through one's participation. I graduated and received my Master of Education degree, but I did not student teach. I had, however, completed my required internships at the designated schools before I could apply to student teach.

The bottom line: I had my master's degree but no certification to teach. Every public school system refused to consider me because I was not certified to teach. However, in that state an individual could apply for a professional five-year teaching certificate after teaching successfully for three years. First-year teachers can be fired within two years without cause because they have not been tenured. As an uncertified teacher I would have to teach an additional year and, then, perhaps teach an additional three years before I would be tenured. This path would take me six years to be tenured. I thought that would be plenty of time for the educational system to determine if I had demonstrated my ability to do the job. During that time I would be paid my fair wage for doing my fair share of the work. No one listened.

Lesson learned: Reality trumps logic, even sound logic.

I was undeterred. Somehow I needed to teach successfully for three years to get my five year teaching certificate. The solution presented itself in the form of a Roman Catholic archdiocese. I procured a teaching position in an inner city Catholic middle school. I could teach under the archdiocese's general certificate to run a middle school. I taught there very successfully for three years after which I applied for and received my five-year professional teaching certificate. While employed by the archdiocese for seven years, I became a curriculum coordinator and then acquired a position as the principal of a kindergarten to grade eight Roman Catholic school.

Lesson learned: Living Robert Frost's "The Road Not Taken" and the road "less traveled by" skinned my knees, blistered my feet and strengthened my bones, muscle and fortitude. My pay for working in the archdiocese, however, was forty percent lower than the lowest paid county in the state.

Lesson learned: there is an economic price to be paid for enlightenment. True learning, that is true learning of the most important lessons cannot be purchased with money. Such learning, it appears, is had by bartering some skin, blood and personal sacrifice.

So what exactly is my work history? While my overall professional career is that of a professional educator, I started earning my own money at a very young age with a newspaper route when I was about nine or ten years old. The town in which I lived during my early years was very small and a boy with a bike, energy and dependability could make allowance money by delivering the daily newspaper to local houses each afternoon. I did so for a couple of years. At this time the climatic pattern was such that during the winter three or so good snowstorms happened during the school year such that schools were closed for a day or two. My middle brother and I would grab our shovels, shovel off the sidewalk in front of our house and then be off to knock on doors and offer the same service to our neighbors for a small fee. We were very quick and very energetic. Sometimes we made about $30 to $40 which we split 50/50. Our parents did not have much money (if any) to spare for an allowance for their three sons so we had to find ways to get what we could on our own. In the summers, this same brother and I would go around the neighborhood looking to cut people's grass for a bit more money than shoveling snow off sidewalks. A third source of childhood money for me was the local golf course where I would shine shoes, clean golf clubs, and caddie. The golf pro at this club was very kind to me. He always took me as his caddie in tournaments at local clubs (clubs in the area and surrounding states) that were within a car's round trip journey. I never went to overnight tournaments. He paid well for the day's activity.

Somehow, when I was going on fifteen, I stumbled into an opportunity to work for a relatively young man who was building a boardwalk on his property facing the bay side of a local resort town not thirty miles from my home. I had been developing a liking for carpentry and would eventually take three years of what was known then as Industrial Arts classes (better known to students as "shop class"). These classes were offered in the college prep public school program. There were more concentrated courses offered at the Vocational Training School for students who were not aiming to go on to college but to enter the marketplace right after high school graduation. The two reliable skills with which I had a degree of proficiency were crosscutting a board and pounding a nail without bending the nail too often.

This individual was an army veteran and lived alone. He was quite confident and seemed to have more confidence in me than I had in myself. His manner, however, put me at ease regarding my insecurities. My first day at work, he showed me how he wanted the boardwalk built. After showing me how to use two nails as spacers between boards to allow for water drainage, he asked if I had any questions. Having voiced none, I was left unsupervised to do the work as he turned and walked off. I did not see him again until around midday when he called the lunch break. We spoke briefly while we ate and then off again to work until quitting time. He paid me every day at the end of the work session. As I did not have a license, my mother had to drive me to and from work each day. This job lasted two and a half weeks or so. I was sorry when it ended.

Shortly after this job and after earning my lifeguard certificate from the local chapter of the Red Cross, I was hired as a lifeguard for a local, private swim club. I worked at this swim club every summer until the beginning of my sophomore year in college. As a lifeguard, I began teaching very little children how to swim. The Red Cross began sponsoring these swimming classes. I enjoyed swimming immensely but all of my early swimming experiences were mostly in the ocean or in the river that flowed through the city park.

In fact my first swimming lessons were taken in that river. My grandfather, his brothers and most of my uncles on my mother's side earned their living as ocean fishermen. It was very important that all children on my mother's side knew how to swim early. That being the case, my mother continued the tradition by enrolling all of her sons for Red Cross swimming classes that took place in the city park. A concrete embankment was erected part way on both sides of the river allowing for a partitioned section of the river to be used as an area for public swimming watched over by certified lifeguards. This is where the swimming lessons took place and this is where I failed my beginner swimmer's final test. The day of the test, unbeknown to all present, would be the day of my near drowning experience.

Throughout the beginner swim lessons all students learned how to swim across the river from one bank to the other. We practiced frequently to improve our swimming muscles. If I got tired then I could tread water, get a deep breath, hold it and go underwater until my feet hit bottom to push off hard to resurface with arms rested a bit. Off I would go to finish my trip. Before the final test was administered, all swimmers had successfully completed the journey across the river quite a few times. The object was for everyone to pass the test.

Whether it was planned or whether it was mere coincidence, the damn up stream had been opened the night before for whatever reason and the river downstream was muddied and swollen. To my young eyes it just looked muddy but I did notice that it seemed different in some other way. My general nervousness about having to perform well was heightened a bit at the river being visually different. Only one swimmer would swim across at a time. My turn came and I dove in confidently; but, somewhere in the middle of my swim, I decided that I wasn't going to make it. I needed a bit of a rest. I did my usual procedure to find the bottom to push off somewhat refreshed. To my surprise, as I went under the water, I could not feel the bottom as I had on all previous times. So, instead of resurfacing, I continued to wave my arms underwater to go a little more downward to find the bottom that I was sure was just out of reach. There was no bottom to be found. I was out of air. I wouldn't be able to push off the bottom to get back to the surface. I began to swim frantically for a gulp of air. I got to the surface but not in a controlled fashion. I grabbed a gulp of air, smacked the water surface and went back down under. Everything went black. The next thing I remember was lying on my back looking up at all the faces looking down at me. The lifeguard asked me if I was ok. I said "Yes," and sat up. It wasn't until much later, probably after I became a Water Safety Instructor, that in recalling the incident, I knew I had nearly drowned. Lifeguards are very important people.

I learned how to swim well, but my family could not afford any membership to a private pool. My town did not have a public pool. The river was the public swimming area, but my mother loved the ocean. The ocean and the breaking waves were my watery playground. My brothers and I would body surf the waves or swim out to sandbars beyond the breaking waves. Swimming in the ocean made me a very strong swimmer. My favorite stroke was the breaststroke. I could easily see all of the landscape when leisurely swimming the breaststroke. I was the breast stroker for the club's swim team and then became the Red Cross Water Safety Instructor.

Having earned the required certificate, I was authorized to teach and train Red Cross certified lifeguards. Eventually, I became the manager of the swim club. I was pretty young to be managing any enterprise and was fired from that position because of a dispute between the owner of the club and myself. The Red Cross certification to become a lifeguard had mandatory requirements for earning the certificate. One such requirement was time training in the water. Some members of the club's swim team had conflicts between competing for the team at away meets and lifeguard training sessions. I took an unyielding position that these team members had to choose between competing or lifeguard training. I was not going to certify any individual who did not have the required hours of training in the water. My position was that I had the responsibility to make sure that the lifeguards I trained would not end up in a double drowning situation because they did not meet every requirement mandated by the certificate that would carry my signature as endorsement. Team members and their parents were very unhappy. The owner and I had a heated discussion and I was fired. I did not take this firing well. I do not like to fail, but life goes on and I was young. My career wasn't over. It hadn't really begun but the wages that I earned at the swim club were very substantial for summer employment needed by a struggling college student.

Actually, reflecting upon that experience now, I had begun my career as a teacher. I was a teacher of little children who needed to know how to swim so that they would not accidentally drown. The career path that I would eventually choose for myself would be that of a professional educator. The confrontation between myself and the owner of the swim club would not be the last time I challenged the position of the authority residing in positions of power. It would also not be the last time that I had to face the consequences of confronting those in powerful positions.

The summer after my sophomore year, I worked pumping gas at a college buddy's family-owned gas station that was located just outside of the resort where I built that boardwalk when I was fifteen. Pumping gas earned me a minimum wage and free boarding at the gas station. I was not able to save any money that summer but was able to support a summer at an oceanside resort town for my one-time summer vacation. Otherwise, all of my summer employment served the purpose of earning money to help pay for my college expenses.

The summer pumping gas, while not being economically robust, was nonetheless extremely beneficial in a truly educational sense. My boarding accommodation was quite sparse. I had a room in the back of the gas station. My college buddy was married and their accommodations were more robust. Not to worry, we all got along and the summer was more for relaxation at a fine summer resort with a beautiful ocean beach of pure white sand than seeking to establish a display of high social standing above our peer group. Every summer this resort town was populated with many, many fellow college students doing likewise.

Of the many lessons that I learned that summer, one stands out as being more burned into my psyche than any other. Growing up thirty miles or so from this resort town afforded my family many, many trips to the public beaches. When I was older and had my driver's license, I could, on a warm summer's night, grab two blankets off of my bed; jump in the family car at my disposal; drive to the beach; throw one blanket on the cool white sand; lie down under the cloudless sky with a full moon; listen to the gentle breaking of the waves on the shore, and fall asleep perfectly safe. Others were doing the same. There were several campfires along the beach in either direction from where I chose to lay my head. Of all of my experiences growing up, these nights and my camping trips to oceanside parks are the most glorious.

Life situations change especially when opportunities for amassing wealth present themselves to individuals who have the power to exploit. This ocean resort town was not very developed when I was growing up. Vast sections of the beach were sand dunes and no buildings. The oceanside boardwalk went only to 9th street. Most families brought picnic baskets. There was only one arcade parlor on the boardwalk and a small assortment of vendors. Almost all came for the beach and ocean swimming.

This summer of my sophomore year was drastically different. Oceanside hotels and condominiums stretched beyond the original nine streets of the original boardwalk that is now over two and a half miles long and ends at 27th Street. During that summer I was chased off the beach at dusk by beach patrol personnel who informed me that the city had passed an ordinance that banned sleeping on the beach at night. A fleet of huge earth moving machines would be driving along the beach to sift the beautiful white sand and rake up all of the debris that the day's visitors had left strewn for miles littering the beautiful white sand. At the same time a fleet of bulldozers would be driving out into the ocean past the shoreline to push sand back up onto the beach. This resort town was built on a huge sandbar and it is the natural consequence that sandbars are moved by wave action and the flow of the current. I was told that army civil engineers were hired to combat the natural erosion of the beach. I also discovered that hotels and condominiums had been allowed to designate the beach in front of their respective buildings as off limits to nonresidents of their properties.

Lesson learned: The wealthy and powerful inherit the earth (not the meek) and will rent the earth to those who can afford it so that the wealthy and powerful can become more wealthy and powerful.

I have not revisited nor do I ever intend to visit that resort town again.

I finished my undergraduate degree in English Studies and tried to get a job at a newspaper but the newspapers were all folding, leaving many journalists with experience looking for the remaining jobs. Desperate for some kind of job, I began scanning the want ads for employment prospects. I happened upon some catchy ad and went to see what was what. It would be my first and last experience as a salesman.

How appropriate is it that a college graduate with a B.A. English degree starts his salesmanship career by selling "the world's best, extensive, unabridged dictionary" door to door? I was fresh out of school; my cushion money was quickly running out, and Baltimore was not cheap. Thus began my excursion into the world of sales.

During the first day of orientation, it was made clear that the job was to sell a product; that salesmanship was not truly dependent upon the product being sold; that a good salesman, a really good salesman, could sell anything, and that this particular product was an excellent, unabridged dictionary with a finely crafted, beautiful binding. But this product (it was reiterated) was not the issue at hand. The issue at hand was the process of how the product would be sold.

"We've paid an excellent firm who hired some very fine psychologists to research the best way to sell this dictionary. This process was developed and tested and works very well. What you will be learning is how to sell this product to the targeted consumer group. But before we do that, we want to explain to you what being successful in these sales will do for you."

It was explained to us that at the beginning while we were learning how to sell we would be earning a moderate base pay and commissions on what we sold. The real money, we were told was in the commissions. Each presenter that day spoke of his first day with the company; how he sat in the same seat as we were sitting in now, and how they advanced up the company to earn the excellent pay they now received and the unlimited prospects that lay before them.

Each of us newcomers would be under a mentor. The mentor was highly motivated for each of us to be successful because he would prosper with each of our successes. When each of us became competent salespersons, each of us would take on a newcomer or two of our own. As we gained a few newcomers and they in turn became successful salespersons who gained newcomers of their own to be mentored into competent salespersons, our wealth would begin an ever-increasing momentum upward. This was the structure that promoted the company's rapid growth and profits. A proportion of my commissions would go to my mentor just as I would receive a proportion of the earned commissions of those whom I mentored. In this fashion every individual gained financially from the economic gains of the company. I was never certain about how much of a percentage of the commissions would be passed up the chain and uncertain about how far up the chain those portions of the commissions were shared. This detail, at this point in my development, was not an issue because I had not sold anything and I had no newcomer to mentor. My first challenge was to sell a dictionary to someone.

Each of us was given a small card printed in such a fashion that we could mark off each sale made. The presenters set a challenge before our group by offering a prize to be obtained by the first individual to make the first sale of the group. The prize was defined as a surprise. A second card was distributed to us that had a pledge written upon it that said that the individual who signed this pledge would not misrepresent himself or herself nor the product being presented. This small card would be the critical Achilles heel of my brief experience with salesmanship. At the end of our training period, two days for which we were paid, each of us signed this pledge.

The target group was the managers of the various shops and vendors housed in the mini malls which dotted the given targeted region. The group of us met on the third day at some designated spot from which we would carpool to the first mini mall of the day. Having arrived at our destination, we were given the following instruction:

"You remember that our research for successfully closing a sale is based on how fast you present your "radiation" (sales slips of other managers in the area who ordered a dictionary). Since we are just starting out today, the first thing you have to do is write up your radiation. Pick any random store and make up some manager's name to put on the sales slip. Two or three will be enough to get started. You weed these out once you begin making sales."

We sat down curbside and made up our "fake" radiation. This was not an easy task for me. I was thankful that the situation never arose which deemed it necessary to produce my pledge card. We worked until lunch at which time we debriefed our experiences while we ate. No one made a sale. We were off again that afternoon and still no sale had been closed. We were given a pep talk as we loaded up at our last mini mall and, again, at our original starting point. We left to return the next day at the same spot.

The next day we were two people short. They quit. We were informed and given a pep talk about not being discouraged and that, once we got in the groove, we would each begin to see the orders and money flow into our pockets. "Now let's see who will win the prize for the first sale." Off we went to encounter the same results as the day before.

I made my first sale in the afternoon on the third day. It was a Friday. Another fellow salesperson also made a sale. The mentors were ecstatic. Congratulations were heaped upon us and we were the examples of just how easy it would be for the others to do likewise. "We are all going to celebrate tonight. It will be on us [the mentors]. We will meet at [the name of some night club in Baltimore and its address]. Everyone must come. We will pick up the tab." I went but do not remember the club's name. It was a very, very nice club. The lights were bright and colorful and the music was great. We didn't pay for anything. The bill must have be very substantial. These guys must have been doing pretty good to afford this night out celebrating only two sold dictionaries.

On the following Monday I quit. I was pulled aside and asked what was wrong. I said that I just could not do it anymore. I had signed a pledge not to misrepresent myself or my product. The "fake" radiation was a lie, a misrepresentation. I was told, "No problem. Don't use the radiation until you make a sale." But that was the significant purpose that was repeated over and over again. "You must get the radiation out faster." No, I was done. I thanked my mentor and left.

Lesson learned: I believed that they told the truth. To be a successful salesperson, the product is secondary to closing the sale. Salesmanship is about selling. You have to do what is necessary to make the sale. You **must be able to do whatever is required** to make the sale in order to be successful. I had learned that, at least at that time in my life, I had limits to what I would do.

That done, unemployed again, I returned to the want ads and finally gained employment as the "low man" in the kitchen services department of a nursing home in Baltimore. The "low man" is also known as the "gofer", the person that goes to get or do what he is told by any other person working in the kitchen. I worked in this capacity for a brief time after which the Director of the home called me into his office and offered me the job of Central Supply Manager. My responsibilities were to keep inventory and order all of the medical supplies and other supplies except for those required by the food service department and to stock every nursing station with their supplies on a daily basis. I took the promotion. Central supply management was not particularly difficult. The previous manager had set up a very clear, easy and highly functional system. That being the case, after a brief time of getting acclimated to the job at hand, I completed all of my managerial chores by 1:00 pm if I skipped my lunch break (which I usually did). I could have paced myself and stretched my tasks to last until the workday ended, but I was not accustomed to working that way. After three months, the work was pure routine without any challenge and without any diversity. I was so bored that by the end of the fourth month, all work being done by 1:00 pm at the latest, I began to fall asleep in my office chair behind my desk at the back of the stock room. I began thinking, " I'm just out of school. I've mastered this job. I'm often falling asleep at work. Is this it? I'm going to be doing this for 35 to 40 years? I have got to go back to school and get a career of some type." The very next day I went to see the director and told him that I would be enrolling in graduate school for the next semester and would be unable to continue to work when I went back to school. I left that job amicably and relieved.

Graduate school progressed without a hitch except for one professor and his Behavior Modification class. This time my confrontation with the powerful voice of authority was not a solo engagement. It was a team effort. One of my classmates was studying to get his theology degree. He and I had a problem with the assigned project that would be 50% of our grade. The assignment was to use everything that we were studying regarding behavior modification from B.F. Skinner to present day developments of this particular school of psychology to shape the behavior of one of our unsuspecting roommates preferably one not enrolled in this class. We were to design our program to achieve the targeted behavior that we would shape, collect our data, chart our progress, and write a paper. It was simple enough. However, the fly in the ointment in this particular project was a question of ethics. Free will is not a component of a strict behavioristic approach to behavior modification. The basic premise is that our personality, or who we are and how we act, is the consequence of a series of rewards and punishments and that free will does not exist. An individual's behavior and quite possibly who that individual is or becomes is based on operant conditioning i.e. a system of reinforcements -- rewards and punishments dispensed according to several different schedules.

The eradication of free will did not sit well with my theologian classmate especially when we were commanded via a critical assignment to usurp the free will of another by consciously shaping behavior via clandestine activity. I was not so much offended by the argument over the existence or nonexistence of free will, but I was deeply concerned about secretly manipulating the behavior of another human being, especially as an exercise to see if you can do it. There are other, more ethical ways that we could use to demonstrate our complete and deep understanding of behavior modification.

After collaborating during dinner, we decided that we would take issue with the assignment at our next class. We would both raise our hands and whoever was picked would initiate the challenge. It was a brief exchange with my colleague, the professor and myself. It was only four to six exchanges. The professor ended the challenge abruptly with, "If you want to study ethics, then enroll in Dr. Zepp's ethics class down the hall! Do the assignment or fail."

That was definitive. A choice had to be made. How my English professor had wrecked me! To be enlightened, to be informed, is to be changed. I do not remember him ever explaining how to survive after being enlightened. Thanks loads!

I concocted a plan. I would do the assignment but, to protest against the powerful authority of a college professor, I would hand write in my best penmanship my final paper in number two pencil. This professor always graded papers with a content over style score that would be averaged together. If I carried this plan out, then I had to work very hard to ace the content because I was absolutely certain that he would fail me on the style aspect of my grade. The overall score for my project was a solid C. In graduate school, the overwhelming opinion is that grad students are to never get below a B. This professor had words with me when he handed my project back to me: "Never ask me for any recommendations for anything." This was the only real problem I had in graduate school.

Lesson learned: It is difficult to be true to yourself when authority flexes its power to do you harm.

My oldest brother continued his formal education past his master's degree to earn his doctoral degree. I remember his relating the difficulties that he was having with his doctoral committee. The difficulties appeared to me to be more political and having to do with issues of style rather than genuine exploration and pursuit of academics. It appeared to me, based on what my brother conveyed, that some professors on his committee required agreement with them as opposed to an honest pursuit and alternative inquiry into defensible possibilities.

Lesson learned: The continuation of higher degrees may be absent of true issues regarding free thinking and more about preserving the positions of those in power.

Thus ended my formal education.

Among the multitudinous and diverse power plays that must be navigated well and that speckle the American educational system, one stands out as being most substantial and potentially devastating to myself and my family. This situation arose from my family's migration from our home state to another state and seeking employment in that state's public school system. At the time of transition, I was currently the Director of School Services for a private psychiatric hospital's adolescent locked unit. Based on my experience, my formal education and my Professional Education Certificate, I eventually gained employment as a special education teacher in a public school resource room. While I had certification to teach hearing impaired students, I did not have the specific special education certificate required by our new home state. During the hiring process the State Department of Education was contacted and arrangements were made for me to teach with a provisional certificate while I took the necessary course work required by the state's certification process. During this hiring process, the State Department of Education verbally expressed that I needed only twelve credits which amounted to four courses to complete or something akin to that for my state certification and I also had to pass a teacher performance test required by the state. It was simple enough. I would take course work while I worked full time under a provisional certificate until all requirements were fulfilled. Easy.

But it turned out not to be so easy. In the end, when I submitted my application for my special education certificate, a new review of my transcript was initiated. This new review recommended that I needed to take more course work to gain my certificate. I was not pleased. I met with my Superintendent and my Director of Special Education to discuss the matter. Both were aggravated with the State Department of Education.

I called the State Department of Education and conveyed to them that I had been told that I only needed to take the course work that had been completed. The individual with whom I spoke said that he was sorry, but I was told incorrectly. An appointment was arranged for me to meet with Dr. X to discuss why I needed more course work.

The meeting began well enough. Cordial greetings were exchanged with smiles and handshakes. Pleasant small talk ensued but then I was taken off guard. My file was placed on the desk, opened, quickly scanned and Dr. X raised her head and spoke something along the lines of, "Well, yes you need to take some more courses."

I reiterated that I had been told by the State Department when I was being hired that I only needed the course work that I had just recently completed.

"Well, if you had not chosen to make a career change, then you would not have this problem," was Dr. X's retort.

I was unprepared to hear such a response and l laughed out loud. "Dr. X, you can't be serious. You have a doctorate! I wasn't an electrician or an accountant or anything like that. I was a teacher with a five-year Professional Teacher Certification. I didn't change careers." I should not have laughed but her response just struck me as so absurd. The meeting ended abruptly. I needed additional course work. That was that.

A couple of days later I received a letter from the State Department of Education with a list of all of the courses I needed to take to obtain my special education certificate. It amounted to being just shy of earning another master's degree.

I was once again in a serious dilemma. Do I fight the state and risk losing my job which would put my family in serious, serious economic jeopardy or fold up, comply and do what I was told regardless of how I felt about the injustice of the situation. Had I been single, it would have been an easier choice. Only my hide would be on the line, but being responsible for others who are dear to me makes such decisions much, much more difficult. We had just moved into an unknown area without friends or family. It took me an agonizing couple of days, but I decided to fight.

I met with my union representative, spoke with my Director of Special Education and my Principal. A formal meeting before the Hearing Officer was scheduled, a union lawyer was arranged and letters of demonstrated competency regarding my performance as a resource room teacher were written by the Superintendent, two Directors of Special Education, and two Principals under whom I worked.

At the hearing, the winning argument of the day was delivered by the State Department of Education, "We do not determine competency. We do the course count." Outstanding! The Department of Education is not responsible for assuring competency. Its function is to assure a course count. I left amazed.

Fortunately for me, my Superintendent, Principal and Special Education Director were very supportive. I was offered another position to teach that did not require the State Department to certify for that position. It was a new program under the Title One Chapter level developed at the University of Arizona. It was called Higher Order Thinking Skills (HOTS) which I would teach for many years.

Lesson learned: Take nobody's word, especially individuals with authoritative power. Get everything in writing and signed.

Lesson learned: For authoritative positions of power, competency is not necessarily an issue.

To summarize my work record, I worked these odd jobs along the way before starting my teaching career: construction laborer, life guard, swimming instructor, Red Cross Water Safety Instructor, manager of a private swim club, and an assembly line worker converting minivans into mini-campers. (I wired the circuit box.) Before I began teaching professionally, I was employed as a Psychiatric Nursing Counselor (PNC) for the adolescents and admissions units of a private psychiatric hospital. As a professional educator for 25 years, employed in both the private and public sectors, I worked as a regular education classroom teacher; as a special education teacher in a resource room, and as a Title I HOTS teacher. Most of my teaching experience was on the middle school level, but I also worked as a curriculum coordinator. I was recruited and hired as the Director of School Services at the same private psychiatric hospital where I was once a PNC. I was the principal of a kindergarten to grade eight Catholic school. At the end of my teaching career, I designed, implemented and taught an alternative education program for a public middle school. These are the credentials from which I speak further.

The Need to be Educated

I have explained that my mother was driven by a strong desire for her sons to be well educated which was translated into an unyielding pushing (hounding) for her sons to graduate from college. While I cannot speak of any deep motivation that might have resided in the core of my brothers' souls, my early drive to do my studies in grammar school and junior high was to cope with my mother's high expectations. Whatever my performance in the early years of school, it was not the product of my desire to be educated as much as it was a desire to avoid my mother's tongue lashing. Somewhere along the road to a better outlook on being educated, this early motivation of avoidance of mother's disappointment became a true desire to explore and learn which opened me up to be so receptive to that professor's lecture about enlightenment, information and that muse. When, how and why this transformation occurred is unknown to me. I am not sure if I was aware that it had occurred at all.

I do know that it was never *my* plan to go to college. In fact I did my best to avoid college. Part of that truth was based on my performance in my Catholic grammar school; the nuns' assessment of me as a student; my grammar school grades juxtaposed to my brothers' grades and the like. I believed that I was ill equipped to make it through college. Even though my mother displayed no doubts, I saw it more in the light that my mother was in deep denial about my abilities. During my senior year in high school when seniors are contemplating their next move upon graduating, I wanted to go into the merchant marines.

There was an aggressive side to my mother. I experienced both her yin and her yang. She was certainly an advocate of spare the rod and spoil the child. I was certainly going to go to college, according to my mother, but most of her feedback to me regarding my demonstrated abilities was mostly negative most of the time. I don't remember any compliments. (The feeling that I harbored was that I had done nothing to deserve a compliment. So the fault really was not hers.) There was no basis for me to believe that I could achieve academically. If this is all true, then how do I explain successfully earning my Bachelor of Arts degree in English and my Master of Education degree?

There was one class in high school that was taught by one of the wrestling coaches. He was a big man, 6 feet 8 inches tall or maybe even 7 feet. Back then that was extremely tall. Wilt the "Stilt" Chamberlin was one of maybe two or three basketball players who were 7 feet tall. Seven feet does not seem to be so unusual now. Anyway, this teacher was extremely proficient at making up tests that asked questions on everything that was covered in class and in the readings. I failed a couple of the first tests and did poorly on the next couple. My problem was that I was not studying and only did some of the reading. One time I wised up. I did all of the reading and studied hard before the test. I found that I did very well on that test. It finally struck me that if I did study and did do the work, then I did well, but I had to study. My test grades were rising. I felt good about the change. Working hard for this teacher did not earn me A's but I passed his course with a strong C. This I believe was the beginning of a new path. I began to study in classes that were more difficult for me and found that studying really did improve my school work, but I had not yet developed a good habit of studying all of the time.

The nuns were sticklers on grammar and penmanship and error-free final copies written in ink. We used fountain pens. I never really saw a ball point pen until I entered high school. In high school I discovered that everything that I was taught and learned in my English classes at the Catholic grammar school allowed me to slide in my high school English classes without causing any severe impact on my grade. All of the grammar taught in high school was a repeat of everything I learned in grammar school. The hundreds and hundreds of sentences that were assigned to be diagramed for homework instilled a more than competent facility with phrases, compound sentences, compound-complex sentences, clauses, adverbs, adjectives and so forth and so on. I really did not have to work too hard at the grammar part of my English classes; however, the reading part was still very laborious. My visual handicap was still present and continued to secretly slow down and interfere with the flow of reading novels from cover to cover. My better than average language mechanics (grammar and such) offset my poor performance on the literature end. I could not keep up with the reading so I could not answer some aspects of the books under discussion. That which I had read I had down cold. I used what I had read as much as possible and pushed it as far as I could in discussions and assigned essays. My grades were much better in high school than in my Catholic grammar school.

Even though I was greatly improved as a student in high school, I still did not want to go to college. The war in Viet Nam was very active my senior year. The draft lottery had every eighteen-year-old's undivided attention. My friend, Charles, (really my only friend in high school) and I were going to enlist in the navy together. Together we went for our physicals at the appropriate naval base. My family was not too happy. As it turned out, I was rejected because of my right eye. The physical determined that I had a significant blind side on my right. I also had a severe acne problem which disqualified me. My friend enlisted in the navy without me. I went back to my merchant marine plan.

My mother, my eldest brother and others, whom I don't remember, were doing their very best to nag me into applying to college. I was outnumbered and became overwhelmed with pressure to enroll anywhere just in case I changed my mind. After all, it would not hurt to have a backup plan just in case. I was tired and worn down, so one night I proposed a deal to which there was agreement. I would apply to only one college of my choice and if I was accepted, then I would go; but, if I was not accepted, then I would pursue the merchant marines with their full support.

Soon thereafter, I made an appointment to see the high school guidance counselor. My inquiry was simple, "What local college has the best mathematics program?" I was given the name of the college that, upon graduation, the graduate could go anywhere he desired with a recommendation from the mathematics department. Perfect. Mathematics and the sciences were my strengths, but my English class grades were average and I scored weak on my verbal SAT test. My SAT math score was good but not great. My plan was to apply to that college because I did not believe I would be acceptable to them because the college had a high reputation to uphold. It was a good plan.

It was not a great plan because I was accepted as a Summer-February freshman. This particular college knew that about 5% of the freshman class would not make it past the first semester which meant that 5% of available space would be empty at the start of the spring semester which began the first of February. The month of January was reserved for an explorative mini-mester for students to pursue nontraditional course material such as parapsychology. Therefore, to offset vacancies in the spring semester, the college accepted Summer-February applicants who would take the fall semester classes in the summer and then returned for the spring semester. I was one of the lucky recipients of this special acceptance. It needs to be noted that the summer classes would not be watered down because of the reduced chronological time into which the summer class structure had to fit. Classes were structured as if they were Tuesday/Thursday classes during the regular fall class schedule. Classes were 90 minutes long instead of the Monday, Wednesday, Friday classes which were 60 minutes long. A minimum of 12 course hours had to be completed by the end of the summer. That would be two classes in the first half of the summer and then two more classes during the second half.

I was accepted, so I had to go. The agreement had to be honored, especially since I thought that I had succeeded in what I thought was a clever scheme to stack the odds in my favor. Ok, I was in college. I would take courses as though I was meant to be in college. I signed up for Chemistry for science majors and some other course. It probably was Comparative Religions. The chemistry class had a mandatory lab attached to it which made it a 4-credit course. It was this Chemistry for chem majors that would have a significant impact on my self-image as a viable student.

The first class in chemistry opened with the professor outlining the grading structure for his class. He was a young Ph.D. Rumor among the students was that our professor was around 28. We would all agree soon enough that he was very, very smart. He started out matter-of-factly.

"This is Chemistry 101 for chem. majors. You should know that the median score on tests will be

50. I have already compiled my grade book. Five percent of the students will earn an 'A'; five to ten percent will earn a 'B'; five to ten percent will score a 'D'; five percent an 'F', and the remaining scores will be in the 'C' range. The only part that I have not figured out is whose name to place by each score. That determination will be made by each of you."

Without a doubt, we were to be graded on the curve, the bell curve of normal distribution. We would be competing against each other for our grade. May the best student win. The median score on the first test that we took was a 20. All tests were reviewed in the very next class. After the review of that test, students began forming small study groups to improve their scores, or more correctly, to improve their *understanding* of the material. Two tests later, the median score was 80. The professor was smiling when he handed out those tests and commented, "You did a very good job on this one. I will get you on the next one."

I calculated what would be the grade spread given the data received. In a class of twenty students, the number of A's would be one which meant that the number of F's would also be one. The range of five percent to ten percent would yield a maximum of three students scoring either a B or a D. The remaining students (between twelve to sixteen depending on the number of students awarded either a B or a D) would be the spread for receiving a C.

This class and his follow up class of chemistry (Chemistry 101 and 102) were without a doubt the most difficult classes that I have ever undertaken. I received a C in Chemistry 101 and a B in Chemistry 102. One day when working during a scheduled open lab for students to complete assigned, unfinished or difficult experiments, I asked the professor while waiting for a chemical process to occur, "So, why is it important to you that your tests have a median score of 50?" His response was quite interesting to me and upon careful consideration I could see his point of view.

"My job as a professor of chemistry is to make sure that I challenge every student. Every class always has a range of student talents and abilities. I do not want any of my students to get a perfect score. A perfect score means that I have not set up a situation for that student or students to be adequately challenged by that test."

I decided that his thinking was sound even though it made things very difficult for those of us who were less talented.

Lesson learned: There are benefits to competition.

When I left that first class where the grading parameters were explained and after the professor smiled and said that he would get us on the next test, I said to myself, "I'm not the one to get that F. He's not going to get me." I was ensnared but I was determined.

After completing my summer school freshman semester successfully (two B's and one C earning 11 credits with a grade point average of 1.64 on a scale of 3.0), I knew that I could do this college thing. I surprised myself especially when I found out that this professor's Chemistry 101 and 102 classes served to weed out the freshman body of those individuals who are not studious enough to maintain the college's standard.

My brothers went to college on athletic scholarships for their abilities playing tennis. I had no such abilities and I was not a shining star academically in high school. My family did not have the money to put any of us through college and my brothers were already in college when I submitted my one and only application. My mother being the determined individual that she was, found a scholarship program for visually handicapped students. She collected all of the necessary particulars and submitted a request in my name for one of those scholarships which I received. That was how my tuition and books were covered.

Sitting alone in my dorm room during the spring semester of my second year, I fumed internally with extreme anger because my scholarship, which was a government sponsored scholarship, was no longer of concern to the government. The funds were cut. My scholarship was gone. I knew that I could graduate from college and that I was not stupid after all. That I had proven I could do the work was of no consequence. I would have to leave college because I was poor. I had no money. The injustice of the situation I felt was great. There was no way that I, or my parents, could find the tuition for this college let alone all of the other expenses required of a college student. I would have to leave. Shit!

I transferred to a college in my home town. I could live at home. The tuition was much less than the one and only college that diverted my merchant marine journey. I was unhappy, to say the least. But things would work out. I eventually obtained my B.A. degree and moved on to earning a master's degree in education.

What is vital at this point in my deathbed reflections is that I wanted to be taught, to exchange ideas in robust discussions, and to learn what I did not know. My mother's wish for me to be educated was eclipsed by my own desire to learn all that I could possibly learn.

But what if an individual, perhaps hidden in some unknown niche of his or her soul, determines that individuals *need* to be educated? *Needing* is distinctly different from my mother's *wanting* for her sons to be educated. It is also significantly different when the individual experiences the *wanting* in his own soul rather than coping with his mother's *deep wishes.*

The need to be educated began to permeate my consciousness when I encountered a philosophy expressed through the understanding of three coins. The first coin from which the other two were developed to fulfill the intentions of the originating coin is called Joe's Honor Coin of Reciprocity:

The evolution of this philosophy began with the mantra inscribed on the back side of this coin. The originator of these three coins professes that this mantra developed as two parts. At age fifteen or sixteen, the originator conceived the first part: "See a thing for what it is; Nothing more; Nothing less." He chose to live by that command from that moment forward. That command, however, proved to be inadequate as a guiding beacon. There was always something fleeting that would then partially emerge only to quickly vanish, a vague something that was just out sight of an individual's perception of the reality before him. The identification, understanding and embracing of this phenomenon as an intricate element of all reality was added and celebrated in the second half of his mantra: "But remember Wonder and Mystery are forever and always present." This full command is more than adequate as a guiding beacon for one's choices in this life.

The front side of Joe's Honor Coin formed as a result of the originator attending a weekend men's retreat. The originator's emotions were already heightened the Friday night of his arrival because of recent events in his life, and the weekend events continued to build in him until all crescendoed to a single occurrence during the Saturday evening's festivities.

He had met a man named Joe who moved him, the newcomer, to feel very welcomed. During the next twenty-four hours Joe revealed publicly and privately his long struggle with depression and the events tied to that potentially debilitating condition. Joe was not the only man struggling with strong emotionally charged consequences of life's dark side. There were others who also shared their secretly endured troubles.

That Saturday evening after dinner was over several men performed unique, creative presentations of their own design. Joe was one of the last to present. It would turn out that Joe had put on several wonderfully colorful and tastefully designed t-shirts, one over top of the other thus camouflaging the array of t-shirts.

Stepping in front of the group of men sitting in chairs to the left and right of a central aisle, Joe spoke of his warm feelings and deep gratitude for the men sitting before him. Then he did something that astounded the originator of Joe's Honor Coin. Joe stepped in front of a man sitting in the front row to his right which would be to the left of the audience and said, "I'd give you the shirt off my back." With that he took off his outer shirt and gave it to the man. The maker of Joe's Honor Coin was amazed to witness such an act. This phrase was a cliché but to see it actually done powerfully impacted the creator of Joe's Honor Coin. Joe turned to his left, walked some steps up the aisle, turned to his left again, and repeated the exact same words and gesture. The emotional state of the designer of these three coins was again shocked. Like getting a booster shot, his emotions went reeling to a new excited state that had to be contained with concerted effort. Up the aisle a little farther, Joe stopped in front of the newcomer that he so warmly greeted and said to the maker of these three coins, " I'd give *you* the shirt off my back," and did so with a warm smile.

It was a beautiful yellow t-shirt with a frog swimming in water with his head above and his legs dangling below the illustrated, stylistic ripples of the water. The receiver of this t-shirt was undone internally but composed externally. He could not speak. Joe moved on, and most likely repeated this act again, but the man who designed the front side of the coin inscribed with his lifelong mantra stopped being aware of the happenings surrounding him. Internally unhinged, he resolved to be civil but to get to his bunk as soon as possible and sleep. The next morning would be to make his fair-the-wells as quickly as possible and with brevity be off toward the safety of one's home before a complete meltdown occurred.

Once home, this emotionally supercharged individual took two days to reflect on this extraordinary event, to confide in his wife, and to try to synthesize what had been experienced. The words: "Truth, Honesty, Honor, Respect," and "Reciprocity" are the nouns that state what was viewed and experienced as the men interacted with each other concerning the significant and perhaps protected truths of their lives. The one verb, "Nurturing" was the predominate activity streaming throughout all actions of that weekend.

Most importantly, however, is the motivation behind the drive to have this coin minted. The creator of this coin felt compelled to reciprocate the honor bestowed upon him by Joe's gift of the t-shirt that as it happened had the image of the first totem in the creator's medicine wheel --a frog. The frog was the first of four totems revealed or recognized by the maker of these three coins around the same time the mantra was first embraced. Frogs are important because they symbolize metamorphosis and change. Frogs change from aquatic tadpoles into land animals who love the water. For the designer of Joe's Honor Coin, the fact that Joe bequeathed him a t-shirt sporting his first totem was a demonstration of the wonder and mystery that is forever and always present. After conferring with his wife and explaining all of the ramifications of the weekend, his experiences and the whirlwind that had impacted him, it was agreed to spend the money to mint the coin and present it to Joe as an honor reciprocated.

Reciprocation is not an act of obligation. Reciprocation is not an act of loyalty. Reciprocity is being compelled to act in kind regarding acts received. It is the action received that motivates the action returned. Regarding the other nouns cited on the front side of this coin the following statements have been made:

> Truth and Honesty are not synonymous. Truth and honesty are not the same entities because there have been, and are times when, an individual must *honestly* say that he does not know the *truth*.
> The degree of *honor* is observable through the degree of *respect* shown. You honor the individual when you show that individual the utmost respect. Honor the lives of others. Honor all life. Honor the planet. Honor all steps to improve.

Genuine *reciprocity* occurs when truth, honesty, respect and honor form the foundation upon which reciprocity stands. Reciprocity is being compelled to act, compelled to reciprocate. I was compelled to produce Joe's Reciprocity Coin.

The need to be educated becomes clearly apparent when Joe's Honor Coin of Reciprocity is deeply probed for understanding. Gaining a deep clarity of the distinction between truth and honesty; respect and honor, and appropriate acts of reciprocity may require the individual to seek as much education (both formal and informal) as can be obtained. Certainly, when mercy, tolerance, stewardship and guardianship are added to the mix, education is not just a desire. It is needed.

The second coin developed and minted is called The Decision-Making Coin.

After living many years with the mantra on Joe's Honor Coin and reflecting upon truth, honesty, honor and respect, the maker of these three coins concluded that all decisions could be traced back to two choices. An individual can either choose to nurture or to exploit. Thus The Decision-Making Coin was first minted on December 21, 2015. Being raised a Roman Catholic, the story of original sin was well known. The Tree of Knowledge, the snake, the apple and the temptation were all known and perhaps understood from an early age. Age and life's experiences, however, contributed to the concept of original sin fading into a smoggy, polluted atmosphere over a once clear understanding.

As it happens often with wonder and mystery, ideas seem to pop into one's consciousness without any known cause. So it was that the epiphany about the nature of original sin crystalized during a discussion (or reading) about ecosystems, niches, trees, humans, eating and Mahatma Gandhi's ahimsa (the reduction of harm to the lowest degree possible).

As human beings high up in the food chain, we cannot survive without eating organic material. We are not primary producers. We are not like trees or the grasses that can take in raw, inorganic matter and, with the aid of the sun's energy, convert that inorganic matter into organic matter used for nourishment that sustains life. We must consume organic material. We must consume life. We have no choice in that matter. It seems quite apparent that original sin, the sin with which we are born, is the condition of needing to consume other life so that we may live. Hence the Exploiting side of The Decision-Making Coin.

Nurturing, however, is a pure choice. It is not mandatory that the individual nurture anything or anybody. Sometimes the motivation to nurture may not be primarily about nurturing but more about exploiting. Consider animal husbandry. The caretaker of beef cattle is motivated to care well for his cattle because he wants a vey good product to eat or sell. The ultimate apparent nurturing in this case is really an issue of exploitation.

Without proving or disproving that all decisions can be ultimately traced to these two choices of nurturing or exploiting, suffice it to say the designer steadfastly believes that all major decisions are rooted in either of these two possibilities. But, to highlight, every individual must exploit to some degree. It is unavoidable. This is the infamous original sin.

There is one other aspect of The Decision-Making Coin that needs to be explored. It was not a mistake, nor was it by chance that this aspect of the philosophy or value system is expressed as a coin. This is a coin that is for flipping. Modern science stands upon the premise that evolution evolves by chance occurrences. Randomness is a key component to our scientific understanding of evolution. Thus the flipping of a coin represents this randomness. An important decision must be made. Do I exploit the situation or do I nurture. Flip, and proceed according to the outcome of the flip.

I witnessed a demonstration of this coin and the flipping aspect of it to an elderly, educated woman. When all was explained and the decision to nurture or to exploit was announced and the coin was flipped to determine what action the flipper would take, she became very angry. "That's not what I do. I don't make my decisions randomly." "No problem," was the response, "You don't have to flip the coin." The subtlety of The Decision-Making Coin is the first decision that must be made. That first decision is to decide whether to flip the coin or not flip the coin. The persons in possession of The Decision-Making Coin may simply turn the coin over to the side of their intention. You can consciously turn the coin over to reveal your choice to exploit or to nurture.

Flipping is not mandatory, but that choice enhances the coin with another subtle characteristic. Each time the coin is deliberately and consciously turned to either the nurturing side or the exploiting side, the owner of the coin will reveal to him or herself the nature of his or her core character. The function of this coin is to reveal the motivations behind the owner's actions. First, the owner, in determining if the decision at hand is somehow rooted to either the nurturing or the exploiting side of the coin, must reflect upon the nature of the choice and the nature of his motivation at each step along the way. Second, when a determination is made as to his or her true motivation, that choice is validated by the conscious turning of the coin. Finally, the owner of the coin can decide to take this coin and throw it deep into a dark corner of his bureau drawer to be forever forgotten. Such a person, however, would most likely never purchase such a coin. While such a person may argue that he or she does not act randomly, such a person is (or wants to be) ignorant of his or her true motivations. This latter statement goes to the heart of the mantra on Joe's Honor Coin -- See a thing for what it is, nothing more, nothing less. That being understood, the individual who is not interested in The Decision-Making Coin most likely would not be interested in Joe's Honor Coin. We are getting at the interconnectedness of these coins.

The third coin has been named, Two Sides of the Same Coin. Two sides of the same coin are inseparable. You cannot have one without the other. Such is the nature of the third coin. Thus the name.

On the freedom side are diverse individuals. Each carries a sign. The woman carries a sign with the words: "Our Petition". The man carries a sign that says, "My Petition". This side is about freedom to dress differently, to think differently, to speak those differences and to live differently. But, are there no limits to the allowable diversity which full freedom seems to indicate? If I am injured, am I not free to retaliate? If I am free to speak my thoughts, can I not shout my hatred and incite others to follow my lead? If I am stronger than others, am I not free to dominate (maybe even enslave) the weak? If I have power, am I not free to wield it to my own advantage and take whatever I want? In short, what checks unlimited freedom?

The check on unlimited freedom is not dictatorship, tyranny, enslavement or the like. The healthy, the nurturing, check on unlimited freedom is responsibility. Free individuals must act responsibly or risk the deterioration of their freedom into descending states of repression. Free individuals must collectively not tolerate bullies. But, instead of attempting to delineate all of the negatives to avoid, consider the image on the responsibility side of this coin. Unlimited freedoms are checked by individuals choosing to help others cooperatively. Freedom is protected by cooperative nurturing. Differences are allowed in a free environment, but all individuals must act cooperatively for the good of all individuals, especially those who are weaker or less talented, less intellectually endowed, or less fortunate in all the ways that other humans are endowed. This responsibility is easily and clearly expressed with this understanding:

> The community of individuals is responsible to nurture and assist each and all individuals to become the best that is in him or her to become.
>
> Each and every individual, to the best of his or her ability, is to assist the community in carrying out its responsibilities.

This is a statement that consciously and deliberately turns The Decision-Making Coin to the nurturing side.

Education, both formal and informal, is a necessity for those individuals who accept this value system as a guide for their life choices. If those individuals open themselves to be receptive of the wonderfulness in the universe, then fulfilling the need to be educated becomes, not a chore, but the source of penetrating joy. I promise those individuals a fully satisfying life experience.

The level of intimacy between individuals living according to the value system encompassed in the gestalt described by these three coins will be unmatched and will deepen and expand as they gain more insight when they experience the ramifications of actualizing this world view.

Education is needed when living this world view to better equip the individual to cope with those who do not prescribe to these ideals. There are intelligent, well-educated individuals who, whether or not they own a Decision-Making coin, choose consciously to turn to the exploiting side most, if not all, of the time. It is my experience that those who are intelligent and well educated who are also devout exploiters are most often successful in their dealings and therefore become wealthy and powerful because they are not restrained by the needs of those persons or situations they exploit. Such individuals are prodigious opponents to those who embrace Joe's Honor Coin of Reciprocity and its companion coins.

It is through formal education that individuals acquire the skills in reading, writing, conversing, calculating, understanding history and science and more, all of which contribute to improving powers of perception and reflection needed to see a thing for what it is: nothing more; nothing less. Additionally, education (formal and informal) is needed for self protection.

While education is paramount, cooperation is equally so. I fear I may not have emphasized enough that cooperation is an essential element for those ascribing to these three coins. My life experiences have indicated to me that intelligent, well educated, powerful and wealthy narcissistic individuals are best controlled by cooperative actions of individuals who profess a world view antithetical to that of self-centered narcissistic individuals, who are devoutly greedy.

My informal education gained from my life experiences on the many school playgrounds that I frequented growing up has taught me that bullying behavior is learned, developed and regretfully perfected as bullying children grow into bullying adults. Discussions and conversations concerning our public education system have not focused on the informal social education that our children receive during their 12 years in our public schools. Discussion of the existence or nonexistence of free will aside, the point of view of behaviorism is that bullying is a learned behavior. Bullies are not born bullies. Bullies learn how to be proficient bullies. They hone their skills on our playgrounds and on our streets and, at times, within the halls of our schools. The bullies on our school playgrounds and in the halls of our schools grow up into adult bullies if their behavior is left unchecked or, worse, their bullying behaviors are reinforced unwittingly.

Consider this perception. One lone bully on a school playground is usually physically or emotionally substantial. On a one-to-one basis, he or she can easily intimidate a weaker child. If the children on the playground see themselves as separate, unconnected individuals fending for themselves, then the bully can rule the playground via individual confrontations with weaker children, developing a climate of intimidation that engulfs the entire playground. On the other hand, if the lone bully is confronted by say ten children acting in cooperation, then the situation is drastically altered. In this altered situation, the bully usually begins to recruit his needed henchmen. If this new situation is left unchecked, then the potential for gang formation grows.

While the above scenario is simplistic in its presentation, it captures what I have witnessed as a child and as a teacher with 25 years of experience augmented with my work with adolescents requiring assistance within a psychiatric setting. What is missing in the above scenario is the role of the adult authority which is mandated to supervise the developing children. This authority function for the general public is mandated to the government and the police. The role of the supervising authority is significant in both cases.

If the supervising teacher or teachers turn a blind eye to bullying behavior on the playground, then the children are left to self protect. Cooperation between the bullied becomes more critical in opposing the bully. If the teachers intervene but the intervention lacks the ability to eradicate the bullying behavior, then the bully gains more power as he or she is seen as being more powerful than the authority. The intimidation factor grows. The cooperation between those being bullied turns to enlisting the authority to their predicament without real success.

In short, to summarize, while I believe in the world view described and implied by these three coins that represent the true relative position of the human individual to the surrounding world of which he or she is a significant and critical part, I believe that there is much more present in that world view than I have yet to discern. Those who seek to nurture as opposed to exploit can best defend themselves against self-centered narcissistic individuals by banding and working together to sustain their ability to live and thrive within their shared world view. Without cooperation, each individual must stand alone to challenge self-centered narcissistic individuals and bullies. There is a great potential that such an individual will have to grow out of the gentleness of a nurturing personality to become more of a fierce self-defender. Cooperative self-defense is a better option.

If I am so confident in this value system and if I have demonstrated a more than adequate understanding of the message contained in these three coins, then why do I need to carry them on my person? Why do I need to be so attached to their physical existence? I carry all three coins with me every time I venture out of my dwelling because of the need for cooperation. I want them available to me to help explain the world view that they encompass. Chance may offer an opportunity to speak with individuals who may understand and embrace this gestalt and who are potentially inclined to this way of living. These coins serve as a collection of banners to be placed upon the field of life around which like-minded individuals may rally. Around these banners, like minded individuals can discuss, nurture and implement actions for growth and self-preservation.

These three coins as symbols, as banners, also serve to be a homing device to which others may outwardly be identified as kindred spirits seeking to abide by a uniting world view. The idea of having some type of symbol to represent a common point of view, value system, code of behavior and such appears to me to be critical to the establishment of a concerted, cooperative effort by a group of individuals attempting to achieve a positive impact on society and the individuals who populate that society. Organized religions have a number of such symbols or artifacts. Corporations have trademarks which serve to represent the company's character as represented by what they say and how they act. These companies will do all that is in their power to assure that this trademark is not tarnished.

I prefer these three coins over religious groups for three reasons: First, because there is no mandate within the world view of these coins that requires homage to any deity, nor any mandatory ceremonies to practice, nor any of the other elements that distinguish a given religion from the secular world. Second, given the first statement, any individual from any religious persuasion may subscribe to the proponents of this world view because there is nothing inherently "evil" or "demonic" in the proponents of this world view. Third, from my limited comparative religion studies, I have encountered all of the elements encompassed by these three coins within almost all, if not all, of the major religions of the world.

To be clear, however, the sentiments in the world view of the three coins as presented here are secular in nature and that is precisely why they are so important. This is about humankind's aspiration to be the best that is the true nature of humankind to achieve. This is about each individual achieving the highest level of humanity possible. This is not about achieving a heavenly reward or avoiding an eternal, horrific punishment. It is about achieving a better life for one and for all, for the living, here on Earth.

Consequences and Foundations

There are varying degrees of bullies and a diverse array of tools and methods that they can utilize which are physical, emotional, intellectual, abstract and tangible. As a matter of fact, anything that is available to those who nurture are also available to those who exploit. The only differences between those who nurture and those who exploit are their inclination or lack thereof for self-discipline and the motivation behind their actions. As stated before, intelligent, well educated, powerful and wealthy narcissistic individuals and bullies are not inhibited by the needs of others and these greedy individuals are not burdened by self-restraint regarding their desires or purposes. To be sure, bullies and exploiters have a range in degree of bullying and exploitation. Some might just steal your girlfriend or boyfriend. Others might con you out of your retirement savings. Still others may take over countries.

I have had the unfortunate experience of crossing paths with such an individual. As per usual, the difference between me and the predator who targeted me was substantial in age, experience, know-how, education and strength. He was in his thirties. I was fifteen.

The individual who targeted me as his sexual interest was the same priest to whom I sought absolution many times in the confessional by confessing my struggles with puberty and a difficult home life so that I could receive Holy Communion during Sunday's Holy Mass. It was some time after I met this man, associating with him and assisting with activities of the Catholic Youth Organization that a situation was developed in which he took me out of my home state to his cottage for a weekend. It was a traumatic, frightening experience.

As soon as I regained the safety of my home, I went to the rectory to see another close friend who was also a priest in my parish. I told him about the behavior of the predator priest and wanted to go to the police. The advice I received was that this offending priest was a powerful man in the Church; that it would be his word against mine; that I would just be hurt again, and that I was assured that this person would never again be able to hurt me or any other boy. This advising priest gave me his solemn oath on the matter. I left the rectory. I never saw the offending priest again. He never returned to my parish. Outside of speaking to this advising priest, I never spoke a word of my experience to anyone else until 45 years later when I went into crisis; sought out help and began my road to recovery which eventually led me to some intensive psychotherapy in the form of Eye Movement Desensitization and Reprocessing (EMDR) therapy. The total time of doing EMDR was about three years.

The first round of EMDR greatly helped to diminish my rage and anger even though fragmented remnants still reside in some hidden recesses of my psyche. The second round of EMDR was initiated after a hiatus from the first round. Once the rage and anger were healing very well, the intense pain and sorrow that the rage and anger shielded became exposed. The emotional sensation felt like everything in my environment was touching the new, raw, unprotected skin exposed by the bursting of my immense bubbles of blistered hatred. This immense pain and sorrow lingered just below the surface of my daily outward appearance. That too needed to be healed.

Many individuals who are aware of sexual abuse and who have never experienced it tend to focus on the sex. In and of itself, sex is not injurious. Ask any consenting adults who share in sexual activity and most will attest to the joy of the experience. Hopefully, the reader can look to his or her own experiences which would verify that sex is not meant to harm but to thrill. The damage which is severe and immense in sexual abuse is emotional, psychological, soulful, and even intellectual. There may be physical trauma as well, but the physical healing is more easily accomplished than the damage done otherwise.

Having reflected upon my own healing and survival of childhood sexual abuse, I have had to face the perceived portrait of the predator. The engagement of these reflections initiated after embracing the mantra to see a thing for what it was: nothing more; nothing less. I think that I do believe that predators and bullies are not born as such even though there is a part of me that resists identifying any redeeming quality in the person who preyed upon me. Narcissistic individuals, however, may have a biological origin that was not their making. There may also be some different biological aspects that effect other uncivilized and / or exploitive behavior. Putting biological issues aside, bullying and exploiting behaviors are learned. If they are learned, then there must be some type of teaching behavior associated with that learned behavior.

[Before I continue, I feel compelled to point out and highlight a previous statement of importance. The need to be educated is at the heart of my ambiguity regarding the true nature of the individual who targeted me for his exploitation. It requires much more than religious brain washing to truly see whatever humanity exists in the person of the predator priest who objectified me as his instrument for his self-satisfactions. My formal and informal education is critical in assisting me to see him for what he is, nothing more; nothing less.]

I have reasons to believe that my mother may have been abused as a young girl which would give rise to the possibility that her early abuse might have been the impetus for her abusive behavior to her sons and her husband. I have survived my mother's dark, cold side and I have survived her bright light, passionate, fiery side.

I am remembering an exchange between me and a very, very close friend (my current wife) who has intimate knowledge of the past abuse by my mother and the predator priest. My wife inquired as a curiosity how I managed to break the cycle of abusing one's children by not doing likewise to my own sons. Some research has found that abused children tend to do likewise later in life when they become parents themselves. The sentiment expressed to me ran along the lines, "It is remarkable that you turned out so well given your experiences." I responded that as an amateur photographer I am very familiar with reading and interpreting negative images. I ascertained that I learned how to live well by learning from the negative images of my childhood. I did the opposite of what I saw and I ignored what was said to be the truth of things. Instead, I decided to search out the truth for myself. Here again is the need to be educated to free one's self from blind obedience.

We are the consequences of the past. The consequences of my parents' upbringing and the experiences of their lives before they met and married along with their shared experiences before my birth forged the immediate environment into which I was born. I am the consequence of all of those interacting forces until I begin to take possession of my own life. At the point of possessing my self, I become not just the foundation of my future but also the future in general.

That foundation was seriously damaged when the exploiting predator priest trashed the mortar and brick and blasted the landscape which I was working hard to keep level and straight. So, the consequences of that individual's past intertwined with my present to become another quagmire of someone else's cumulative history from which I now needed to extricate my self. Ensnared and bound once again, I confronted the potential of becoming the consequence of a life other than my own. At 15, uncertain, without any real assistance, my soul knew no path to take.

I remember the day that I resolved the question of my possible suicide. It was a profoundly pivotal, late afternoon to early evening. I walked to the playground that filled the space between the Catholic grammar school and the Catholic rectory. I sat down on a spot I deemed to be dead center as best as I could discern. This 'moment' started in the late afternoon and ended at dusk after the sun slid away. A four-foot iron fence and gate separated this area from the sidewalk all the way from the north end of the school to the south end of the property of the rectory. The setting sun was at my back. I faced the iron fence. A large cross adorned the peak of the school to my left and faced the street.

First I wept sitting cross legged alone. I was unaware of time. Thoughts swirled. I don't remember each of them but I do remember the general theme. " You may be bigger and stronger and more powerful and may get the best of me. I am not going to help you. I'm not going to do your dirty work for you." [The 'you' was the collective of all those individuals who 'beat me up', my mother, my middle brother, the predator priest, and other bullies. I did not delineate them at the time. The 'you' was a large looming dark force hovering over me on that desolate, empty, greying school yard.] "You may kill me but I'm not going quietly." [An image of me clawing, kicking, struggling while my arms and legs were tightly gripped by some unknown powerful force dominated my internal attention.] "Fuck you!" I stood up and stomped out of the iron-gated past.

The significance of this 'moment' crystalized during my EMDR sessions. I did not recognize it at the time but in treatment it became clear that I was deciding whether or not to kill myself. I decided that I would not "do your dirty work for you." I left resolved and very angry. There was a substantial wind blowing after the sun set. Unzipping my coat and exposing my chest as much as possible, I dared the wind defiantly or the fates to give me pneumonia or something to take my life. I was a child hurt. I was a teenager pissed off.

In treatment we talked about ego states and how an individual who experiences deep trauma sometimes has his development truncated at or near the time that the traumatic event occurred. I left the injured part of my self (the hurt little boy) lying on the ground in the fetal position as the defiant, angry teenager stomped forward to survive as best as he could. I abandoned part of my self and buried it in the deep, dark recesses of my psyche.

This is not the most healthy method for healing extreme trauma, but it was the best that I could do at the time. Forty-five years later I would do a better job. We, each of us, are the consequences of the past beyond our personal time. We are the consequences of our parents' past and the consequences of our parents' history together before we are born. Our parents are the consequences of their parents as well.

This array of the consequences of past events converge in the flow of life's movement into which we are plunged at birth. We did not make the currents that swirl nor the currents that flow. We only keep our heads up, tread water and learn to swim.

At the same time we are the foundations of the future. We are the potential rocks that may alter the flow of past consequences. As we block more and more of those past consequences we build a new river bed for calmer water. We become the foundations of the future when we block the flow of the debilitating consequences of the past which will allow our life to flow in the direction of our choice. We must take possession of our own lives. Here, again, education is a necessity.

We must learn how exploiters and bullies have robbed and are robbing others of a better life. We must learn how to heal the injuries we have survived. We must learn how to work to prevent further injuries to ourselves and others. We have to learn how to make our own riverbed into which the water of our life flows from which our children will emerge and make ripples of their own. Healing the consequences of past traumas that burden our movement is requisite for being a better foundation which alters our future movement. It starts with seeing the true nature of everything and anyone, especially regarding power and wealth.

If exploiters and bullies are few but are wealthy and powerful, then cooperation between the many is critically required. If the many have organized a cooperative effort to contain the exploitive and bullying behavior of the strong and mighty few, then those few will seek ways and means to corrupt the efforts of that organization. Corruption has metastasized in the vital organs of the society in which I live. Who will see this illness for what it is -- not more than it is; not less?

The 'Holy-men' of the Roman Catholic Church (RCC) are Hiding Behind Their 'God'

Disclosure:

Before I get into the gist of this issue, I must highlight a disclosure. My mother attended daily Mass frequently. My brothers and I attended a Catholic grammar school until grade nine when I, as the youngest, transferred to public schools. My oldest brother, however, attended a Catholic high school. During our grammar school years we had to attend a Roman Catholic religion class every day. I received high grades in my religion classes. My other grades were not that good.

The punch line is that at the age of fifteen I was targeted by one of my confessors, a predator priest, seeking gratification for his sexual preferences. I did not receive professional treatment until 45 years later when I went into crisis concerning my experience of abuse from that priest to whom I confessed my 'sins' struggling with puberty issues. Thus, I am not neutral about child sexual abuse.

Gratitude:

I am so pleased to witness persons and institutions not connected to the RCC shedding their fear of the RCC and treating it as any other institution is treated. Teachers, psychiatrists, psychologists and other individuals who work confidentially with others are not exempt from reporting their concerns about harm that might be, or has been, perpetrated on others especially when children are involved. These individuals are known as mandatory reporters. They are obligated to report to civil authorities their concerns and/or knowledge of possible criminal activity regarding personal harm. The RCC says that the 'holiness', the confidentiality, of the confessional is sacred. Wrong. If a religion wrote dogma that under certain circumstances, an individual may kill another person for breach of religious law (say adultery), then would the civil law against murder be overruled by the sanctity of 'sacred law'? Is God, via the confessional, the protector of criminal activity? The theology of the above stated sanctity of the confessional relegates God as the protective cover for those who prey on children (and others) thereby escaping civil accountability for their deeds.

What is Not Explained to the General Public:

The confessional was never a place to enable the repetition of serious (grievous) sins. Every single time I confessed my sins in the confessional I was given a penance (a chore) that had to be completed in order to demonstrate my sincere regret for my sinning behavior. The priest determined the penance to be done. Almost every time, I was given a set of prayers to complete: five Hail Marys, the rosary, or attend the Stations of the Cross. It could be anything the priest deems appropriate. Upon this point, the RCC can take a critical step in protecting children, preserving the sanctity of the confession and helping the souls of the sinners get to a heavenly reward. The Pope and in turn the RCC can decree that all individuals hearing confessions and providing absolution to those confessing child sexual abuse (or any sexual abuse), regardless of his or her station within the Church, must, as a penance, report their offense to the civil authorities. The person hearing the confession does not break the 'confidentiality' of the confession; but, the sinner does not escape true atonement for the sin because he or she must face the civil consequences of the behavior. This would be an appropriate penance for those who commit child sexual abuse or any other serious crime. The RCC agents could then support the 'sinner' as he or she endures the path of his or her appropriate atonement via the civil response to the grievous matter of the behavior.

Some church officials and/or theologians may refute this suggestion as inappropriate because others may decide not to confess such a sin for fear of the civil accountability and thus the soul would be lost to Satan. This would be an intellectual illusion. One of the requirements of the individual confessing is to sincerely pledge to never do the sin again. Don't confess the crime unless you are willing to do the penance. Don't confess your crime to avoid corporal atonement for your behavior and instead be damned for all eternity because you failed to confess a mortal sin. There is a corollary to this mandatory penance: If the original penance (reporting oneself to the civil authorities) was unfulfilled, then all other subsequent confessions would be suspect. The unrepentant sinner having refused to do the original penance would have demonstrated his or her contempt for the sacrament of penance.

I suspect that those in power within the Roman Catholic Church would not go for such a solution for fear that the Church would lose membership. If the penance required by priests in the confessional fit the actual behavior of the committed sin, instead of some abstract prayer that bears no relationship to the actual offending behavior, then how many individuals would ascribe to such a faith? The confessional would no longer be an abstract cover for sinning behavior, especially for repeating the same sin over and over. Is this not a central point presented in Fyodor Dostoevsky's "The Grand Inquisitor"? Is not the true function of the confessional to change one's behavior, change one's life to gain entrance into the kingdom of heaven, and not merely the forgiving of sins (and escaping civil accountability for one's offenses)? Is not heaven earned by one's behavior and not by someone else's pronouncements over another? But, here, at this point, with the pronouncement of this last stated rhetorical question, I open the door to religious believers so that they may retreat into their beliefs. Some would refute:

> "God's law is above Man's law. Peter was given the power of Jesus Christ to lead His Church here on Earth. Jesus said to His apostles, (Matthew 18:18) 'I assure you, whatever you declare bound on earth shall be held bound in heaven, and whatever you declared loosed on earth shall be loosed in heaven.' And again in John 20: 22,23, it is written: 'He [Jesus] breathed on them and said: 'Receive the Holy Spirit. If you forgive men's sins, they are forgiven them; if you hold them bound, they are held bound.' The power of God is with all priests via Peter and the Apostles as bequeath by Jesus, Himself. If the priest forgives, it is forgiven. End of story."

I stand corrected. Behavior has nothing to do with getting into heaven. The magical pronouncement of words are all that is needed so long as they are pronounced by the designated individual.

This is a serious trap if not a significant flaw of the 'religion' professed by the RCC. If an individual's sin (criminal behavior) is wiped out by some pronouncement of 'sacred words' by appointed (anointed) persons then individuals are freed from all earthly consequences of his or her criminal actions. Theologians could argue that this same procedure occurs every day in our courts. A group of 12 men and women pronounce the guilt or innocence of the individual or individuals being tried. Pronouncements are made. Individuals go free.

Decisions have to be made. Again we arrive at a point that highlights the need for individuals to be educated. To make an informed decision regarding the sanctity of the confessional over the protection of our children requires individuals to be as educated as possible to think through significant, critical issues and to evaluate conclusions made that are pertinent to the issues at hand. At the same time these educated individuals must respect and be open to the wonder and mystery of life's experience and be open to the fact that we cannot know everything that needs to be known. A strong education is needed to perceive that the pronouncement by 12 jurors after a trial with the public display of evidence and arguments is not the same pronouncement made by a lone priest over an individual confessing alone in secret, in a lightless confessional.

One of the cultural mores that permeates the RCC is that a mortal sin (thus a sin provoking eternal damnation if unconfessed) is committed if an individual 'brings scandal upon the Church'. This is how this works in the mind of a child: 'If I accuse a holy person of a very bad act (touching me sexually) I will bring scandal upon the church'. The sinning behavior is transferred from the predator to the victim. To compound this problem, the parent, who is informed by the child of the abusive action, is faced with the same dilemma: 'Do I report this accusation and bring scandal upon the church?' Or, does this parent simply respond to the child: 'No priest would ever do such a thing. He is a man of God.' Remember also that this parent has received the same training from his or her earliest years and so the training is well engrained in the psychological profile of the parent. This mandate to "not bring scandal upon the church" is hugely beneficial for maintaining secrecy from secular eyes.

There exists another element that fostered the years (decades) of child sexual abuse and coverup. The infallibility of the Church is intimately entangled with the fact that the Church is made up of humans and humans are not infallible. This dilemma allows for an interesting side-stepping dance. The Church doesn't make mistakes; the humans in the Church make the mistakes because after all God is perfect and God in His Three Persons (the Father, the Son and the Holy Spirit) is perfect, infallible. If the body of the Church is infused with the Holy Spirit; how could that body (the collective body of the Church officials) allow and participate in the perpetuation of the vast violation and tragedy of pervasive child sexual abuse for decades on an immense scale by the very body that is infused with the Holy Spirit? Answer: It wasn't the Holy Spirit; it was the individual church official who made the mistakes. It was each individual who perpetrated the sexual abuse; it was each individual who was bringing scandal upon the Church and it was each individual who decided to protect the Church from such scandal by covering it up and shipping the abuser to another community of children, and it was the individual who decided not to tell the receiving parishioners that a child sexual abuser was entering service to their community. All these individuals acted as individuals who, unfortunately, sinned and didn't feel the presence of God.

While I understand this position in human terms, I also understand this response as a pat answer of a human attempting to avoid or minimize responsibility, accountability and the admission of a grievous 'mistake'. I also recognize that if it was truly a mistake, then the error occurred by some accident or lapse of understanding. Such a response seems to imply that these actions by the Church were not deliberate and consciously undertaken. The longevity, the global scale, and the vast number of the known victims of these protected perpetrators of abuse belies any statement or implication that this was done unconsciously or without deliberation. The vast amounts of money spent on lawyers, the public relations spinning of responses, and the maligning of outspoken victims, etcetera over decades, all speak to the conscious, deliberate attempt to avoid responsibility, the covering up of behavior, and the silencing of any attempt to discover the truth of the matter. The RCC, the Pope and all others who ascribe to the pat answer described above are trying to have it both ways -- the infallibly Perfect, and fallible humankind (capable of great evil).

As a corollary to this terrible tragedy perpetrated within (if not by) the Roman Catholic Church (RCC), there is a book, *Fallen Order,* by Karen Liebreich (copyright of 2004 and first printed in Great Britain by Atlantic Books, an imprint of Groove Atlantic Ltd). On the inside of the jacket for this book, the reader is given a synopsis of the text:

> For hundreds of years the Piarist Order of priests has been known for its history of important contributions to eduction, science, and culture. Throughout Italy, Spain, and central Europe, the order's schools evolved from shelters created to educate poor children into exclusive private academies. Thousands of children were educated at Piarist schools, including Mozart, Goya, Schubert, Victor Hugo, Johann Mendel, and a host of astronomers, kings, emperors, presidents, even a pope. Yet in 1646, the Piarist Order was abruptly abolished by Pope Innocent X, an unprecedented

step not seen since the Knights Templar were suppressed for heresy in the fourteenth century.

Fallen Order is the stunning story of how the sexual abuse of children, practiced by some of the leading priests in the order, led to The Piarists' collapse.

This corollary is important because *Fallen Order* demonstrates that the contemporary tragedy of child sexual abuse within the RCC that first exploded publicly with the Boston Globe's exposé regarding the Boston Massachusetts Archdiocese in 2002 was *not the first time such an organized sexual abuse tragedy occurred inside the RCC*. The journalism efforts by the Boston Globe research team of journalists was made into the movie, *Spotlight*, (2015). After viewing the movie, muster up all the remaining fortitude that you have left and sit through the scrolling of the list of the global extent to which this terrible tragedy metastasized in your lifetime.

Remember that all of what you viewed in that movie is what is known. This represents the victims that are known. I, being a survivor who has shared with other survivors, know of others who have not come forward. There are many that are unknown. If the RCC had its way, we would all be unknown. Finally, a significant accounting that has never been reported for whatever reasons (difficult to research, no one cared to document, and so forth) is the number of suicides related to this tragedy. I know of at least one. Other survivors have conveyed to me that they know of others. The number of those exposed to this tragic occurrence is huge. Take just one individual survivor and seek to understand the depth of the black hole into which the soul plummeted in order to grasp the damage done to the individual and you begin to grasp the magnitude of the destructive power of this tragedy.

Quantitatively, the said total magnitude of this horrific tragedy would be the number of individuals plus the depth of each dark hole.

Given this understanding I want to return to the reflection that decisions have to be made in spite of our inability to know all that is pertinent to the significant and critical issues at hand. The decision that has to be made regarding governance is whether 'sacred' law should rule over 'civil' or 'secular' law or vice versa. Is this decision to be made based on pure emotion? Is it to be decided upon one's pure intellect?

I contend that neither pure intellect nor pure emotion should rule any decision. I stand squarely, confidently and steadfastly upon all that Joe's Honor Coin encompasses. We must see a thing (an issue, a person, a reality) for what it is; nothing more; nothing less, knowing that there is much we do not know or have only a fleeting vague perception of its being. We must incorporate our suspicions -- whether they have validity or whether they are our biases or prejudices trying to sway us from the truth we do not want to see or whether they are our intuition recognizing subtleties of understanding triggered by something mysteriously perceived by something in us that is unknown to us consciously. We must nurture ourselves and others in the virtues of Truth, Honesty, Honor, Respect and Reciprocity. A critical component for achieving a high standard regarding this aspiration is acquiring as much true education (as opposed to 'training') as possible.

Human history must be considered when deciding which has dominion -- civil or church law? History has recorded religious practices that appease or gain favor of the gods through human sacrifice. Should a religion ordaining such a practice in our country be allowed the freedom to practice such a tradition or should civil law prosecute to the fullest of the civil statute against murder? On the other hand can the lawmakers of civil laws pass legislation that confiscates, imprisons or deports members of a religion because the religious beliefs and practices are offensive to the ruling culture? It has happened before. German civil law killed thousands upon thousands of Jewish members because they were Jews. Native Americans were forbidden to practice Sun Dancing. Civil laws have been written by human communities to harass and otherwise make life miserable for individuals who practice a religion considered to be unacceptable to the ruling culture.

When considering the question of the governance regarding sacred law and civil law, we are ultimately struggling with the nature of the reality we designate with the term "community". What makes a community a community? The heart of the community is the value system around which the community is built. While many small communities may be formed within a much larger community, those smaller communities cannot deviate with extreme significance from the core principles of the value system around which the larger community is built. In a larger community which has religious tolerance as a core value, the tension between sacred law and civil law is resolved via the civil court system which interprets the community's legislated decrees.

Regardless of the decision regarding the dominance of civil law or sacred law, the common element which determines prejudice, double standards, injustices, and atrocities etcetera is the human character. At the core of all communities, religious or secular is the human individual acting collectively. Prejudice, double standards, injustices, atrocities, exploitation and bullying et cetera are human motivations precipitating the actions of human creatures regardless of the robes that they wear.

How the Individual is Critical

I first wanted to title this section, "*Why* Is the Individual Critical," but changed my mind. Some part of me resonated with an intuition that pursuing the path to understand fully the "why" of something is strewn with many wonders and mysteries. Pursuing the "how" of something is more concrete in its perceptive pursuits. This understanding is like trying to get a handle on the behavior of a designated individual. I can more easily perceive what the individual says and does rather than deeply perceiving why he or she does or says what is put forth. It is the difference between knowing the true motivation and knowing the behavior. Behavior is more easily perceived than the deep internal motivation of the behavior. This is not to say that coming to understand the motivations behind behavior is unimportant. Quite the contrary is true. It is simply easier to perceive behavior and verbiage (written or spoken). Motivation and true intent are perceived through the perception of behavior over time and is more an issue of discerning the truthfulness and genuineness of the individual through the consistency between what is said and what is done. Perceiving or understanding motivation and intent is less direct and involves more interpretations and speculations. Thus, I have decided to reflect on *how* the individual is important.

I disagree with Plato's philosophy presented via Socrates. My recollection of my studies in college regarding Plato's dialogues of Socrates facing off with his opponents is that good was perceived as all virtuous. The nature of goodness, the virtuous, was without any trace of evil. This is not how

Hinduism or other religions of the East depict the nature of good and evil as personified by their deities. I choose Shiva as an example. Hinduism's Shiva is the god of creation but also the god of destruction. If you consider good and evil as opposites as + and - are opposites, then creation and destruction are also opposites. According to my reading of Plato, good does not encompass any of its opposite. Since the Greek culture is considered the foundation upon which western civilization is built and Hinduism is considered an eastern religion as opposed to western religion, then Plato's dialogues serve as a point of demarcation between western culture and eastern culture. If one wants to claim that Hinduism is more of a middle eastern entity, then let us move to the Chinese yin-yang (the union of the light and the dark). The point is that western culture and eastern culture are distinctively different regarding the nature of good and evil in that western culture has separated them whereas eastern culture has them united.

This is important because in Christianity, a western religion, the god and the devil are opposing entities at war with each other. They are opponents seeking to rule the other. We, as creatures of human flesh, must contend with Satan and his demons or God and his angels as they vie for control over our actions which serve to define our character. From a human's point of view in the western culture, evil in the world is a disembodied powerful entity seeking our demise. Our name for this disembodied evil is Satan (among others).

This construct of a disembodied tormentor, deceiver or tempter is incorrect. Deceivers, tempters, tormentors, bullies and exploiters are human individuals working solo or in cooperation with others. This understanding is fundamental and critical to hold accountable the evil permeating our world. The old adage "The devil made me do it" must be forever and absolutely dismissed as voodoo medicine for the ills of a sick and suffering individual, community, society or culture. We must no longer look beyond ourselves, our neighbors and other humans for the behaviors that harm life and the motivations from which those behaviors arise.

Rest assured that I clearly understand the profound consequences of altering the nature of evil as western culture has so defined it for thousands of years. If we do not see a thing for what it is, nothing more, nothing less; then we make a serious mistake equal to the mistake a doctor makes when misdiagnosing an ailment and thus prescribing the wrong medication needed for a cure.

Evil does not reside outside the character of the individual. Evil acts are not perpetrated by some disembodied entity. Evil acts are committed by human creatures. The individual does the act that causes the harm. But what about temptation? Where does the temptation originate? The individual who is tempted to perform some action is temped from somewhere and from something.

Granted, the first issue to consider is the determination of the source of the temptation. The source may be from outside the individual who commits the act. As demonstrated by Iago in Shakespeare's play *Othello*, the temptation comes from some other individual who whispers in the ears of others, setting them to do harmful deeds. This sinister whispering will lead to tragedy.

Temptation is not direct action but a solicitation or seduction for motivating others to act. In understanding that the individual possesses in his or her core both the positive and the negative then the temptation is the stimulation of the negative tendency in those who are tempted. However, if the part stimulated is the positive side of the individual then that individual is deceived by the tempter and the naïveté of the deceived character is manipulated by his or her supposed friend. At some point in this scenario a tragedy occurs. Usually in Shakespeare, this tragedy is the death of one or more characters.

If the source of the temptation initiates from within the individual, then the negative side of that individual becomes activated and continues to self-stimulate the individual's negative side. In Iago's case, his hatred of Othello is stimulated by Cassio's promotion over himself. Hatred is the negative side of the positive-negative core of all individuals.

The particulars, the different array of details and affected players, are not the significant issue. The core issue is that acts of evil or acts of goodness are not rendered by disembodied entities. They are the product of 'inter-' and 'intra-' human actions (see Howard Gardner's interpersonal and intrapersonal intelligences). If this is your understanding of reality, then evil in the world is contained or restrained by the strength of the positive side (or good side) of the individual. If the tendency to deceive, to tempt, to torment, to bully or to exploit, etcetera is countered by the positive or good side of the individual, then evil in the world is reduced to the degree that each individual has developed self-discipline.

How is the individual critical? Answer: The individual is the critical first line of defense for containing the harm done in the world.

No longer do humans have to deal with a disembodied superhuman nemesis of peace and good will on Earth. It is within our power to defeat this foe, but to do so we must first understand the nature of our enemy. The individual can gain intimate knowledge of this enemy because if we see ourselves for what we truly are, then we will see the enemy that resides within each of us, but we must see ourselves for what we are: nothing more; nothing less.

Western Christianity states that each and everyone of us is born with original sin. While Hinduism, Buddhism, Jainism and Gandhi ascribe to the practice of *ahimsa* (doing the least harm to other life), no individual can escape *himsa* (violence done to other creatures) in the strictest sense of doing no harm. I learned about *ahimsa* when reading about the life of Mahatma Gandhi. My recollection of his description of *ahimsa* was that the individual works diligently to reduce any and all harm to the very least amount possible. In my reading I remember being informed that there are some Eastern holy men who try to eat only a few, very few, grains of rice each day to reduce any harm done to any other life. This encountering of *ahimsa* informed and transformed me to see with clarity the nature of original sin which escaped me for all of my training and practice of the Roman Catholic religion. Not being primary producers, we must consume other organic material (other life) in order to sustain our own life. There is no choice in the matter. It is our nature to do so. It is how we were created. Each and every one of us was born with this condition. Whether it was consciously chosen or not, portraying the act of original sin to be the eating of an apple was a stroke of genius.

Is this 'evil'? No. But gluttony is one of the seven deadly sins. To see and understand the effects of this condition to mandatorily consume other life for what it is (nothing more and nothing less) requires some education. A child is not born with knowledge nor with understanding. A child is born, becomes hungry and seeks to eat. It is that simple to the child.

I no longer have much use personally for the word 'evil' when trying to understand the harm and 'wrong doing' that permeates the world of humans. I understand correct actions and incorrect actions; creative actions and destructive actions and many other paired opposites that have much more clarity than the generic 'good' or 'evil'. In some cultures or societies that which is 'evil' is embraced as 'good' and vice versa. So, good and evil have too much subjectivity in the interpretation of their nature.

There are two words which have more meaning that more clearly states the nature of harm and the lack of peace in the affairs of human kind -- naïveté and ignorance. Naïveté is 'a lacking of ... (experience, wisdom or judgment etc.)' while ignorance, to my understanding, is formed from the verb 'to ignore'. Thus ignorance is not a synonym for naïveté because ignorance is the 'turning of one's back to what is known.' Ignorance is the ignoring of what is known. Distinguishing the realities of naïveté and ignorance in this fashion allows for a clearer understanding of how naïveté can be more easily resolved than ignorance.

If the individual's action is the result of naïveté, then the resolution is to educate the individual in such a way that the individual acquires the appropriate knowledge to act better. The presumption is that once the individual is appropriately knowledgable then he or she will act better. However, if said individual does not act better after being informed and being now knowledgable, then the resolution to this situation is a bit more involved. The newly informed individual is no longer naïve but is now acting ignorantly. This act of ignorance is more willful than acting naïvely. Ignorance implies a choice whereas naïveté is not a matter of choice. Naïveté is a condition of being.

To choose to deceive, to tempt, to torment, to bully or to exploit, etcetera knowing that peace and harmony will be disrupted and that harm may very well ensue, is to choose to ignore the elements that facilitate peace and harmony. What would motivate such a choice? Motivations as opposed to overt actions are more complicated with numerous and various elements that may have culminated in the choice to ignore the maintenance of peace and harmony. The issue critical to this reflection is that both naïveté and ignorance are solved through the process of education and that the education needed to resolve naïveté is less difficult than that needed to resolve ignorance.

What I have learned thus far in my life is that evil is not the activity of some disembodied entity but the actions of an individual human or the actions of humans in concert with one another. Each individual's character is the union of both the positive (good) and the negative (evil). Since there is no disembodied evil (a disembodied negative entity), and since this negative is under the control of the individual, then Satan (or whatever name it bears) can be contained or controlled. The negative residing in one's character is no more powerful than the positive which likewise resides in that very same character. This can be easily understood as the similarity between -5 and +5. The unit of magnitude (strength) is the same. It is the direction that defines the distinguishing quality.

The condition of original sin professed by Christian religions of the Western culture is the condition with which all human life is born. Each and every person born must consume organic life to sustain its own existence. Each and every one of us must eat life to live. We have no choice in the matter. Each and every one of us must exploit to some extent in order to live.

Nurturing, however, is not mandatory for our life. We do not have to nurture in order to live. Nurturing is pure choice. Nurturing is required by adults only to assure that human babies live and thrive. It is important to understand that if the offspring is not nurtured until it is able to fend for itself, then the preservation of the species is highly at risk. No doubt there exists some mechanism within the nature of the species that enhances the desire within at least one of the parenting adults to nurture and care for the offspring for some length of time until the newborn can attain the ability to care for itself. Thus there is most likely a mechanism that enhances the desire *to choose to nurture* as opposed to abandon one's offspring. It is equally important to understand that the life of the adult parent is not dependent upon its nurturing or not nurturing the offspring. If the parent does not exploit other life so that the parent and the offspring can consume the organic matter needed, then both the parent and the offspring will die from starvation. Exploiting is mandatory whereas nurturing is a choice and the degree of nurturing is a choice from zero to as much as is humanly possible.

I, like every other human creature, have a character composed of the same pairs of opposites that define all human creatures. I am not special. I am not any better nor worse than anyone else. Everything that has been said about the nature of humans and about harm and destruction and choice and the need to be educated and the nature of nurturing etcetera is true about me. I am (like every other individual) the consequences of the past and I am (whether I want to be or not) the foundation of the future, especially concerning my children and all of the children with whom I interacted during my professional career as an educator.

How I am part of the foundation of the future is determined by how I contend with myself as the consequences of my past. I have indicated that I am an adult survivor of child sexual abuse perpetrated by a Roman Catholic priest. I was targeted, groomed, and exploited by this "holy" man who was at least twice my age when I was 15 years old. He is one of the consequences of my past. His actions harmed me to a significant level. Hatred manifested as rage and a very strong desire for physical revenge. The particulars of the multiple ramifications of this unfortunate consequence of my past remain with me to this day in spite of my earlier desire to have all of that part of my self metaphorically amputated. When I finally engaged professional help, I learned that one cannot cut off a part of one's psyche and throw it away. There are many ways to try to wall it off and bury it deep, deep, deep down inside your being (as I did), but it will fester, grow putrid, bubble and fume and will begin to seep out through every crack in your imperfect barricade.

Raged and horrible violent revenge is the opposite of love and caring support. The negative side of myself was definitely stimulated and activated. Rage for me was such an intense feeling to hurt someone so badly that at times I would lose sight of any target. I just wanted to lash out blindly, furiously and uncontrollably. Being in such a condition without a target upon which to vent increased my frustration that added to the emotional stress that ate away the metaphoric landscape of my soul to form an ocean of black, bubbling anger ready to spew forth at the first appropriate opportunity. If there is no target to pummel, then one must create or construct a target. Lucky for me I did not take that path, but rage and vengeance need to cause suffering somewhere. I remember the late afternoon when I contemplated suicide. Obviously, I decided against it. Readers must understand, however, that if rage and anger are not released outwardly, they turn inward and cause harm to the self. Rage and anger do not go away by themselves.

Unchecked and unhealed I would have just continued the exploitive, bullying, negative actions that had targeted me by that wolf in sheep's clothing. The positive side of my self developed enough and became strong enough to form a more positive than negative individual even though I harbored very poor self-esteem and displayed significantly defiant attitudes toward authority figures. Overall I coped well on my own until I had to seek professional help 45 years after my traumatic event when the scandal of Boston's Archdiocese broke in the

Globe and I read that the RCC was professing such overwhelming surprise at the allegations as if they were absolutely unaware of the reported abuse. I knew that this feigning was a lie because I had informed church officials of my predator priest 45 years or so before it hit the Boston papers.

With the help from other positive individuals, self-determination and self-discipline, I contended with my highly stimulated negative side and chose to empathize with others who had a similar life experience, to stand, not for personal revenge, but beside others struggling to contend with being targeted by exploitative or bullying behavior. I stood when appropriate upon my own battle line with bullying individuals occupying positions of power who believed in course counts over competency. I stood my ground with bullying graduate professors who split learning and education into small sections of thoughts organized as separate entities which could not and would not be influenced by other areas of thought like individuals who separate the food on their dinner plates and become enraged when some peas migrate into the potatoes and the gravy runs all over the plate contaminating everything. I finally stood my ground before the Roman Catholic Church and professed what was perfectly clear -- that officials colluded with and protected predator priests over the welfare of children; that it is apparent that the Church was more concerned about its reputation than the lives of the young boys being exploited by the very men that they officially anointed as "holy men" and that the Church has, pretty much to this day, acted like a billion dollar company working diligently and strenuously to keep its trade mark free from any unsightly blemish. The Church to this day refuses to open all of its records to independent criminal and legal professionals to conduct an independent research of the Church's actions regarding sexual abuses by church officials and/or staff. No doubt some readers may detect some anger lacing my reflections regarding the Roman Catholic Church. If none is detected then I am grateful. If my anger is detectable, I am unapologetic. My anger is justified, appropriate and deserved.

But to be a healthy, nurturing, beneficial foundation, I must not seek to pass on the negative consequences of the past. This is done by minimizing the activity of my negative side and enhancing the activity of my positive side. Additionally, I must recognize that I have a negative side and that it is my responsibility to contend with that side of my self. Each of us, even those of us whose actions are perceived mostly as extremely positive, has a negative side and a positive side that forms the whole of the human character.

To Educate...or...to Train

My official retirement was June 2004. I began my career as a professional educator in September 1979, but I was paid to teach swimming lessons to non-swimmers and to train lifeguards when I was 15. That is a combined 38 years of being formally engaged with students needing to learn what I was hired to teach. During those years I have attended my share of workshops, training sessions, conferences, college classes in various educational departments and numerous faculty meetings and parent conferences. As a professional educator, I have worked in the public sector and the private sector. I have been a regular classroom teacher, a special education resource room teacher, a curriculum developer, a principal, and a director of educational services for adolescents housed in a psychiatric hospital. Along the way I have developed some strong views on the many aspects of education. Having taught in many different work environments, I needed to develop the skill of meeting the requirements of each different situation while staying true to my beliefs about the responsibility, ethics and inherent obligations of adults nurturing students.

I was not the only one with strong views concerning the education of children. I venture to say that every adult connected to a child whom I have encountered from the time I started teaching swimming to this day has his or her strong opinions on education. Every employed teacher must find a method of maintaining his or her personal integrity within a workforce teeming with emotionally ladened opinions regarding how the child should be educated. There are scores of books on this topic. In the final analysis, however, the truth is that from the time students take their seats in homeroom at the beginning of the day until homeroom at the close of the day, it is the teacher standing alone in front of his or her class of 20 to 30 students that determines the outcome of the day's events. Education, good, true education, is a cooperation between the teacher and the student(s). First of all and foremost, education is an experience in cooperation. Cooperation can be achieved in multiple ways -- from the cooperation found in authoritarian dictatorships to the cooperation found in responsible and nurturing democracies.

Again we are at a juncture for making a choice. What will be the foundation upon which our education decisions are to be made? Should we use the Decision-Making Coin and flip to determine our choice between exploiting or nurturing, between authoritarian dictatorship or nurturing democracy? Or, should we ignore the need to determine which foundation to use and just jump and tease out all of the particulars of our educational system? Or, do we choose to skip randomness and consciously choose the foundation upon which we want to build? Once we have processed all of these actions, we no longer act randomly because we have delineated with clarity the possibilities we face before we take whichever action we choose.

I am in favor of deliberate action based upon conscious choice. Between exploiting and nurturing, I choose nurturing.

Is our mission a choice? Do we choose to educate or do we choose to train? Or, a), is educating or training the outcome of all of our other choices (if we chose to act by choice), or b), the outcome of our random actions because we chose to ignore the choice in front of us, or c), we simply acted without being aware of the option between educating or training? Simply delineating these options, let alone considering each and every one, demonstrates (once again) the need to be educated.

Since these options have been formulated, consider this: In authoritarian dictatorships, citizens need only to obey. In such a situation, citizens only need to be trained. Creative thinking is allowed only within the narrow confines of the parameters acceptable to the dictatorial rule. Free thinking is absolutely taboo (unless you absolutely keep your free thoughts to yourself). If the level of cooperation is that of an authoritarian dictatorship, then training is the foundation upon which the educational system is built.

Based upon the description of the above paragraph, and because of my understanding that the human character is a whole entity composed of pairs of opposites such as a negative and a positive side; an exploiting side and a nurturing side; a dictatorial side and a democratic side, I choose a foundation based upon educating over training. But what does that mean? How is educating different from training apart from the required adherence to strict obedience? Are they opposites?

They are not opposites. Educating involves some training but training is not the focus. Training is not about educating. If training has some elements of educating those elements are kept to the bare minimum. Educating is about free thinking whereas training, for the most part, is not. Educating is about facilitating the ability of students to see a thing for what it is: nothing more; nothing less. Dictatorships do not like to be questioned and do not like to be scrutinized by the citizenship. Therefore, investigations into social constructs are trained not facilitated, are controlled and tightly censored. In dictatorships students are trained to do 'it' the way they have been told how to do 'it'.

You may have begun to perceive that my understanding and perception of educating over training is tightly connected to my understanding of the three coins. I concur. I choose nurturing over exploiting and so educating offspring is about nurturing children's facility with Truth, Honesty, Honor, Respect and Reciprocity. Educating children is about facilitating them to see a thing for what it is; nothing more; nothing less but know that wonder and mystery are forever and always present. While you aspire to see something or someone for what it is and who he or she is, you will never be able to know absolutely everything there is to know. That being true, it is important to expose students to nonlinear elements and chaos theory if only to reinforce the complexity, wonder and mystery of The Universe. Educating is also about Two Sides of the Same Coin -- Freedom and Responsibility. Being two sides of the same coin means that you cannot have one without the other. To live freely means that each individual needs to be responsible with his or her freedom. The individual needs to be educated to understand that he or she should choose to limit his or her freedom for the good of the community and to work with the community to facilitate each and every individual to become the best that humanity can offer. Educating is not about getting a job and amassing wealth. Educating is about the job of becoming more informed, more in the spirit of learning, and being enthusiastic about metamorphosing into a better you.

Training is instructing. Consider language acquisition as a means to understand the difference between instructing and educating. Learning the conventions for punctuating the written word is an activity of instruction. Sentences begin with a capital letter and end with a period for a declarative statement, a question mark for a question, and an exclamation mark for an exclamation of feeling, and so forth. Matters of punctuation are matters of instruction. Facilitating self-expression and situations to stimulate free thinking while highlighting issues of cooperative actions within a community is educating. To further the idea of facilitating self-expression as a matter of educating as opposed to instructing consider that the poet, e e cummings used punctuation (what there was of it) in unconventional ways.

Remember the professor in graduate school with whom I bumped heads over his segregation of ideas and concepts into neat regions whose borders were absolute barriers between regions of thought, like people who use metal or plastic picnic plates that have little barriers to keep the different foods separated on the plate? What he wanted was a demonstration of his instruction of the efficient use of the mechanics of behaviorism to shape the behavior of an unsuspecting, targeted individual. It is very much like asking students to write a lengthy essay to demonstrate the correct use of punctuation. He did not want and he shut down any discourse on the ethical issues surrounding the application of those mechanics. To my thinking, I conclude that he acted more like an instructor than an educating professor.

This failing might not be entirely his fault. I am reminded of Ralph Waldo Emerson's oration, "The American Scholar," delivered before the Phi Beta Kappa Society on August 31, 1837.

> Man is not a farmer, or a professor, or an engineer, but he is all. Man is priest, and scholar, and statesman, and producer, and soldier. ... The state of society is one in which the members have suffered amputation from the trunk, and strut about so many walking monsters, -- a good finger, a neck, a stomach, an elbow, but never a man. ... the scholar ... In the right state, he is, *Man Thinking*. In the degenerate state, when the victim of society, he tends to become a mere thinker, or, still worse, the parrot of other men's thinking.

When scholars isolate ideas and concepts into ridged regions whose borders are absolute barriers between regions of thought, then they have not heeded Emerson's 1837 warning. When schools and education systems divide the day, every day, day after day, into the four basic subject areas of English, mathematics, science and history with other periods of time allocated for gym, band, art, etcetera, then they have reinforced the notion that ideas and concepts are isolated clusters with limited relevance to each other. What does English have to do with mathematics or vice versa? Mathematics has some important relationship to science but what does science really have to do with English?

During the school year of 1991-92, I participated in the "Critical Skills Institute" presented through Antioch/NewEngland Graduate School. During the introduction to this institute it was explained that educators and business individuals were gathered for a retreat to collaborate regarding the needs of business and the teaching experience of educators to formulate the best educational program to develop a better work force. Twelve areas of learning were delineated from this retreat. There were:

Problem Solving	Cooperation
Decision Making	Collaboration
Critical Thinking	Management
Creative Thinking	Leadership
Communication	Independent Learning
Organization	Documentation

What is immediately striking about this list is the absence of the categories: English, Mathematics, Science, or History. I was extremely impressed with the Critical Skills Institute and resolved to integrate all that I learned into my classroom activities as much as possible.

A strong opinion that greatly influences my view on educating over training is that we, homo sapiens, are nature reflecting upon itself. This activity of nature reflecting upon itself is what truly differentiates homo sapiens from all other creatures on this planet. In prehistoric times our ancestors inhabited Earth much like all of the other animals; but, along the way of the passage of time, we hominidae began to distinguish ourselves from other animals. Our opposing thumbs were a significant departure from other creatures that facilitated our tool-making activity. The moving of the voice box to its current place was significant to our language development. There was another development that is less concrete and more difficult to perceive especially in its early, early emergence. Our ever expanding and more keenly penetrating consciousness is as important as our opposing thumbs or our spoken language.

Evidence of tool making is chronologically arranged by carbon dating artifacts obtained from archaeological digs. Written language can also be chronologically arranged by the same methods, but the spoken language is a wonder to be imagined. Consciousness can be only surmised by the interpretation of the collection of artifacts studied because consciousness is abstract and internal. Consciousness hovers over and quietly permeates our current discourse on the mind-body (brain) reflections.

There are two artifacts that impressed me as a glimpse of the emergence of a displayed consciousness -- one was a simple face outlined on a small stone and the second was simply a human hand print on a cave wall. My recollection is that this cave painting looked as if the artist simply crushed up some brown-red pigment, put his or her hand on the cave wall as a stencil and somehow spray painted that pigment to leave a hand print of the human to endure for thousands of years. This ancient cave painting reminds me of the graffiti on concrete overhangs or country roadside boulders or phone booths: "Henry was here" or "Betty was here". This behavior seemed to me to demonstrate a sense of self as distinguished from a sense of others, a value of the self publicly displayed to profess the beginnings of self-reflection. Consciousness was on display.

Education is to facilitate the development of the best of what we are as an individual and as a group. How language developed is a different question from why language developed and, yes, the general issues regarding the attempt to answer a why question as opposed to answering a how question has not changed in the least. Interpretations and speculations will be unavoidable and will be, more than likely, the predominate elements structuring my point of view.

Speculation: if Homo sapiens evolved in a manner that facilitated the development and the expansion of consciousness, then is it not also possible that an expanding consciousness would seek or gravitate toward tools which would facilitate that development and expansion? Does not language greatly facilitate the exchange of one person's consciousness with that of others who attempt to make their perceptions, interpretations, speculations, observations and judgments etcetera known? Language is the medium through which conversing occurs. It is my understanding that this speculation from the first grunts and gestures to the vast and diverse communications of contemporary society is the general framework in which all Homo sapiens have progressed.

If this speculation is close to being accurate, then the most important function in educating the individual is to facilitate a broad and deep understanding and proficiency with communication; not the study of English. Framing the educational program around communication would be advantageous because such a structure would break down the artificial barriers separating one field of study from all other perceptual pursuits.

All human expressions are forms of communications. The visual arts are a form of communication. Dance is a form of communication. Music, mime, poetry, business letters, law briefs, speeches and jokes are all forms of communications. Mathematics and science are forms of communications. If there is communication then there is a medium through which the communication flows. This medium is language. The language of music and the language of business letters for example are not the same language. The language of the communication must conform to the communication being transmitted but all languages have the same two required components. The communication must first be encoded by the sender into the language of the communication and second the communication must be decoded by the receiver of that communication. The degree to which the encoding and decoding is a mismatch is the degree to which communication is confused and misunderstood. Educating individuals about the process of communication is to facilitate clarity and efficiency in the communication process. Thus, *the dominate area of education should be communication*. The goal of education should be educating (not training) individuals to become multilingual individuals. By that, I mean facilitating fluency in the language of the visual arts, music, dance, writing, speaking, mathematical thinking, scientific investigation, leadership and so forth and so on. I embrace the 12 areas of focus listed by the Critical Skills Institute over the traditional core subjects of English, mathematics, and science and history.

At the heart of mastering these twelve areas of proficiency is the expansion of the individual's consciousness. To me, the process toward mastering each of these twelve areas of focus is an ever expanding feedback loop in which consciousness needs to expand to facilitate progress toward mastering each area. With each step along the way consciousness grows and becomes the catalyst for new insight that improves proficiency in that area. With improved proficiency, new awareness occurs which expands consciousness that continues the feedback loop spiraling to new levels of expanded consciousness. Educating is far more powerful than training.

We, the People; Institutional Pillars of the Community, and Corruption

The democracy of the United States of America is succinctly described in three simple words that says all that is critical to democratic rule -- "We, the People." Governance flows from the People, not from some of the People, not from the rich, not from the poor, not from the powerful, not from the weak, not from a select few and not from one party or two, but from *all* of the People. Governance flows from the whole of the nation, The United States of America; from the whole body of the People via the conscious design of having one person cast one vote in the secrecy of the voting booth. That is the heart and soul of "American democracy" taught to me in my civics class many years ago while a freshman or sophomore in high school. Later, during my senior year, I expanded my understanding of issues concerning our democratic rule in a class named Problems of Democracy. The junior high and high school curriculum have changed much since my high school years of 1965 to 1969. During my adult years, I have witnessed both parties and any number of special interest groups as well as private individuals "game" our system of democracy for the purpose of winning any given election. Gaming the system has taken many forms -- purging voting lists, telling lies, passing laws to make it more difficult to register to vote, gerrymandering, and other voter suppression tactics as well as passing laws that allow the very wealthy to contribute overwhelming amounts of money for the candidate of their choice and legislation that was interpreted to mean that a company has the same rights as the individual citizen.

In a democratically governed society, education must be democratic. Educating (as opposed to training) every individual to his or her highest potential must be one of the most primary concerns if not *the* primary concern of all democratically governed societies. All are to be equally educated. While communication should be the overall encompassing core in which educating activities are performed, there are many other critical efficiencies to be developed within the character of each and every individual populating a truly democratic society and therefore cannot be overlooked. Educating is critical because the health and stability of the democracy is in the hands of each and every individual just as the choice between the negative or positive or the choice between destroying or creating or the choice between exploiting or nurturing is determined by each individual. The personal responsibility of each individual required to protect the freedom of democratic rule is the critical expression of Two Sides of the Same Coin. This coin represents the idea that it is primarily each individual's responsibility to utilize self-discipline to limit his or her personal freedom through the choices that they make.

Educating means facilitating what each individual needs to best decide whether to lie, cheat and deceive or to be honest. This honesty is manifested in the public statement, "Honestly, I do not know the truth of this matter, but I must decide what action I must take which I honestly believe is the right thing to do." Educating means facilitating each individual's ability to decide what path to take: to disrespect other individuals, to ridicule, to insult, to defame, to slander, to dehumanize, demean and abuse them, etcetera or to respect each and every individual and through this respect honor them. Educating means to facilitate each individual to decide whether to take from others without consideration or thought or to instead be moved to reciprocate the kindness, assistance, and other benefits received from others and the community in general. In short, educating means facilitating the Decision-Making activities of each and every individual to choose how to use their individual freedom.

Just as the individual is the first line of defense against the negative forces which we all carry attached to the positive forces within our character, that same individual is the first line of defense to either protect our democracy or assist in the erosion and demise of our democratic way of living -- via his or her personal vote. Thus, educating each and every individual is paramount to our society's health and stability.

Education is about the ability to make good decisions. Education is about being capable of perceiving honesty or deceit, between perceiving truth or fabrication, between respect or bigotry, prejudice, and all forms of disrespect, between honor or contempt, loathing and hatred and between reciprocity or narcissism. And, critically important, educating is about facilitating individuals capable of perceiving con artists and deceivers when it comes to deciding how to vote.

We, the People, have allowed our precious democracy to morph into such a monster. At the close of 2018, I am witnessing an incredible occurrence. Is our democracy crumbling into rubble from which will rise an authoritarian, if not a totalitarian, state? I wonder if I am not watching my country developing along a path similar to the rise of Nazi Germany. Don't take my word for this questioning perspective. Do your own research and read up on how Germany evolved into the totalitarian state that used violence to promote political will, that killed millions of innocent people, and ultimately controlled the whole of the German nation allying itself with Mussolini's Italy and Hirohito's Japan.

I am looking to the midterm elections of November 6, 2018 to see the will of the People. The voted will of the People is a concrete demonstration of the character of the People.

What perceptions of the current state of affairs must be evaluated at this time? I have already written about the corruption that has infected the Roman Catholic Church. What other corruptions are perceivable within the institutional pillars that are supposed to provide stress-bearing support for our society?

Citizens United

The normal path for individuals seeking to become lawyers traverses through four years of undergraduate studies to acquire his or her B.A. or B.S. degree. Next these graduates take and hope to score well on the entrance exam into law school. Upon graduating successfully from law school, they face the daunting task of passing the bar exam. Once the bar exam is successfully completed a practicing lawyer is created. This required path which every lawyer takes is important for understanding my concerns about *Citizens United* and all the legal bantering that has brought us to the current atmosphere surrounding the elections of our government officials. It is also important that to become a judge requires additional effort and to become a United States Supreme Court judge requires even more fortitude and work.

We, the common everyday citizens of the United States, are not so trained in the laws of our land. However, we, the common everyday citizens, form the greatest proportion of "We, the People" than all of the lawyers and judges combined. So, this is not a legal brief. It is an open discourse with any and all of the common, everyday citizens of the United States who care to participate. I am sure that many fellow citizens wonder as I wonder if our legal system is broken or, at very least, suffers from a serious need of a complete tune up and a change-out of all oils, lubricants and other fluids that facilitate the efficient humming of our legal and law-making engine.

Citizens United and all of the legal verbiage, opinions, briefs, counter briefs, arguments and judicial decisions revolve around the "gaming" of our process of electing our government officials. That being the case, we should seek the basic structure of our democracy. As I wrote earlier:

> Governance flows from the whole of the nation, the whole of The United States of America; from the whole body of the People via the conscious design of having one person cast one vote in the secrecy of the voting booth.

All else flows from this premise. What is attached to this basic premise is the right to freedom of speech. We, Americans, hold the freedom of speech as dearly as we hold our right (and responsibility) to vote secretly and without intimidation or the sinister menacing, or usurpation of that right. It is too obvious that our individual vote is our power. Our individual vote is what distinguishes our country from a dictatorship or authoritarian rule. Since we, the People vote, those who want to control the government must control the vote. Hence the "gaming" of the voting process. It is really that simple. *Citizens United* is part of the process of "gaming" our process of electing our government officials.

The power of governing flows from the individual. Unions, corporations, and all other organizations are composed of individuals but those unions, corporations, and all other organizations are not individuals themselves. One person, one vote means that the position of each and every union, corporation, and any other organization is the collective position as defined by each vote cast by each individual of that group. The chairman of the board, nor the CEO, nor the Pope, nor the president of any other organization can cast the collection of votes of all of the members of that given organization. No collection of individuals who come together for cooperative action forms a human being. Such a collection of individual humans does not make up an entity equal to the entity that has been labeled "a human being". A citizen is a human being. A corporation, union, or any other group is not a citizen. Thus, those entities that are groups of individuals are *not the exact same entity* as an individual citizen. Being significantly different in reality, groups of individuals do not constitute "a citizen" and therefore do not have the same rights as an individual citizen. The Roman Catholic Church, Amazon, Google, Target, Walmart, the NRA, the Boy Scouts of America, the Baltimore City Police Department, etcetera do not cast a vote in any United States of America election for any government office.

When the Ford Pinto vehicles were exploding because of a design flaw that put the gas tanks in a vulnerable position and many people died because of this design flaw, the board of directors did not get charged with any crime and no member of the board went to jail. If the Ford Corporation is like an individual, then the charge of involuntary manslaughter should have been considered as a real possibility for the board of directors and the CEO to face. But in the case of the exploding Pinto vehicles, the Ford Corporation is not considered to be a single person upon which such a charge could be hung.

When our ability to think abstractly travels so far down the road in pursuit of ideas, we become more and more vulnerable to lose contact with what is the genuine aspect of our reality. We become very brilliant in our ignorance.

Our laws and the thinking of our law makers may have traveled too far down the abstract path chasing ideas to promote their own personal agendas instead of truly trying to problem solve our many difficulties through a cooperative action as citizens of the United States of America. Instead, some members of some group forming a faction of the populace (special interest groups) formed a brilliant communication based on profound ignorance.

Within the verbiage that surrounds the issue of *Citizens United*, I came upon the following pronouncement:

> "Spending is speech, and is therefore protected by the Constitution — even if the speaker is a corporation."

Again we have lost contact with what is real about our reality. Is it not obvious to every ordinary citizen that spending is not speech? If spending is speech (spending = speech), then speech is spending (speech = spending). I go into the grocery store, pick up a loaf of bread and walk towards the door and make a proclamation, "I have taken possession of this loaf of bread, position is nine tenths of the law, I now own this bread," and I walk out unafraid because speech is spending. RIIIIGHT! That's not going to happen. Spending is not speech and speech is not spending even if some legal pronouncement tries to make it so.

This kind of trap occurs when educating is divided up into rigid compartments of thought which have little or no influence upon each other. We model this falsehood for our young citizens from kindergarten through the twelfth year of their education. Consider the linking verb "is" and the mathematic symbol "=". The captain is John. John is the captain. These two sentences are exactly the same. Mathematically expressed this idea would be: "captain = John". Mathematically speaking equations are the same in both directions therefore "John = captain" is exactly the same (in both directions). Our legal thinking and our law making have strayed into the realm where abstraction has abandoned the true aspect of our reality.

Let us assume that I am like the little Dutch boy trying to put my finger in the dam to keep it from failing. I, as a single citizen, have little power or I control not enough power to alter the legal powers that are the reality of my country. However if spending is speech and every citizen has an equal voice in the establishment of my government, then every individual citizen has the same amount of voice (speech): one person, one vote. There is absolute equality in the premise: one citizen, one vote. That same equality must therefore be extended to all speech pertaining to all elections. Thus no one person nor entity can spend more than any other regarding the equality of voice when considering the election of government officials. Otherwise, one individual's or entity's voice (vote) is more valuable than all of the others. Of course I know that all of this is argumentative. Decisions have to be made. I am once again back to the three coins and the individual as the first line of defense against the negatives and for the positives while knowing that exploiting cannot be absolutely escaped and nurturing is not a requirement for surviving. In this predicament, I believe it is vital to aspire to see a thing for what it is: nothing more; nothing less, acknowledging that we cannot know everything that is needed to be known. We must however act, act randomly or act consciously.

Laws are a matter of words. Just as the Roman Catholic Church has ceremonies in which a designated individual speaks words and makes a pronouncement bestowing sacred reality upon secular reality (as in anointing the thumb and forefinger of both hands of a male adult along with other actions of the rite making the secular man into a holy man), words and oaths are taken making ordinary citizens into lawyers, lawyers into judges and some few judges into Supreme Court judges. Just as we have witnessed and experienced anointed "holy men" of the RCC preying on young boys sexually, lawyers and law makers are not above temptation and corruption. In 5-4 decisions rendered by the Supreme Court, a citizen or many citizens might wonder how much justice truly permeates that law of the land so rendered by the voting voice of a mere nine individual opinions held by a select few men and women?

Time and time again I have heard officials and individuals of prominence articulate the sentiment: "We are a land of laws," or "We are a country of laws," as a badge of honor and decency over the use of brute force and the sentiment: "Might makes right," as the principle of governance. However, there is a flaw in this false honor of being governed by laws over being governed by the strength of brute force. A critical word is omitted by the sentiment: "We are a country of laws."

If unjust laws are passed then being a land ruled by laws is not a badge of honor. Being a country of unjust laws means that such a country merely legalized behavior which would be consider illegal in a country concerned with justice. Because some behaviors are made acceptable through enshrining them in one's legal code does not mean that laws in and of themselves are the advancement of justice. Consider the following hypothetical. A country has a democratic structure of governance but the voting majority of the people elect individuals who pass unjust laws. Another country is under the rule of a benevolent dictator but he rules in a completely fair and just manner. When considering and judging the presence of justice, structure is not the issue just as the packaging of a desired product is not the determining factor of that product's quality. Packaging is a way to distract consumers from considering the quality or lack of quality of the product being purchased.

In the final analysis, educating individual citizens is about facilitating their ability to determine justice over structure. *Justice is of the highest concern*, but *structure is also of great concern*. Structure is of great concern when the system goes bad and by bad I mean the system begins to devolve into an unjust system of exploitation and narcissistic endeavors of a select few over the health and benefits of the overall citizenship. My read on the history of human systems of governance is that dictatorships are hard to change, especially when they are corrupt and unjust. Violence, bloodshed, great suffering (especially by noncombatants), and uncertainty of the justice of the replacing ruling officials are the major elements of removing a dictatorship. Whereas a strong democratic structure with a healthy incorruptible voting system allows for the possibility (hopefully a probability) of a nonviolent removal of officials who act with a diminished concern for justice. Therefore, structure is about facilitating change. Justice is the defining attribute by which to evaluate governance. Justice is about facilitating the health, welfare and development of the overall body of citizens over a select few. This is not to say that the select few are to be deprived. It is to insist that the select few are not to be enhanced over the deprivation of other citizens.

Democracy in the United States of America has devolved.

It has been devolving for some years now and has demonstrated its lowest level since our current government

was elected in 2016. As 2018 comes to a close:
- A free, independent, credible news industry critical to democratic governance is being compromised.
- Daily fact checks are required to correct what the President of the United States publicly states as facts. The voluminous fact checking being required is symptomatic that our independent free press has been and is being seriously eroded.
- It can be credibility argued that an apparent, conscious plan is being employed to dramatically weaken the independence and credibility of our free press. A major area to consider is the extremely tight relationship between Fox News, President Trump and his administration. Some public figures of note and others who are observers of government activities have put forth the notion that this tight relationship between Fox News and President Trump closely resembles a state-run information news organization (a propaganda machine). What gives credibility to this assessment is the collusion concerning the misinformation (the lies) that President Trump puts out into the public arena. CNN fact checks the President. Fox News promotes, explains (spins) and attempts to sustain the President's misinformation in such a fashion that those other news organizations (like CNN) challenging and fact checking the President are 'fake news' organizations.
  - First, this creates a credibility crisis. Which outlet of news is the individual citizen to believe? Having no other independent information evaluator to settle the opposing reports of the facts of the issues critical to public health and welfare, the individual citizen is

more open to choose what to believe by emotional bias over intellectual or cognitive rigor.

- Second, creating an atmosphere of "You're wrong," and "No, you're wrong," wastes decision-making time and weakens the credibility of the news reporting industry.
- Third, such an atmosphere of pointless arguing elevates the need to have a public educational system that focuses on facilitating critical thinking skills (educating over training).
- Fourth, in such an atmosphere of pointless arguing, individual citizens in leadership positions must decide to speak the facts critical to the welfare and health of the general public as opposed to spinning the facts so that they win votes. When winning votes or raising ratings are the ultimate goal of individuals and corporations, the country, the general public, is wounded because serious problem solving becomes secondary to those individual citizens who occupy the positions critical to the general public's health and welfare.
- Social media (Facebook, Twitter and other such internet exchanges) have begun to replace traditional, rigorous and professional investigative reporting with opinions framed as facts without any serious, high standards or vetting process to determine factual accuracy. Recall the many conversations that you have had around the water cooler at work or with coffee and pastries in your favorite coffee shop.

Now consider how much of those conversations were infused with hard, documented facts as opposed to general opinions stated as facts. The internet has exploded that reality of conversational exchange astronomically. Add to this the fact that there are professional spin-doctors that are paid by various agencies -- governmental, political and private -- to manipulate public opinion. (Russian involvement to weaponize social media is the current hot news item; but, Russia is not the only agency or organization to utilize professionals to tell half truths or to deceive.)

- Julia Carie Wong wrote the article, "How Facebook and YouTube help spread anti-vaxxer propaganda" for The Guardian posted on February 1, 2019 16.20 EST. She writes: "In 2015, Mark Zuckerberg weighed in on an unusually fraught issue with an uncommonly blunt statement: 'Vaccination is an important and timely topic . . . The science is completely clear: vaccinations work and are important for the health of everyone in our community.' " Wong continues with: "But when members of Facebook's 'community' seek information about vaccines on Facebook itself, they may be steered toward unscientific, anti-vaccination propaganda. On YouTube, a rival social media platform owned by Google, users seeking information about vaccines are similarly nudged toward anti-vaccination misinformation, much of it designed to frighten parents, even as a measles outbreak rages in the

Pacific Northwest. The Guardian found that Facebook search results for groups and pages with information about vaccines were dominated by anti-vaccination propaganda, and that YouTube's recommendation algorithm steers viewers from fact-based medical information toward anti-vaccine misinformation."

- Falsehoods abound, are viable, and apparently economically profitable. It is not just traditional news outlets that are under attack. It is truthfulness itself that is being forsaken by professionals that were once upon a time pillars of integrity.

- Gerrymandering and other gaming techniques to manipulate the voting process undermines the spirit of the democratic principles which produced the Declaration of Independence and the Constitution of the United States of America.

  - There was a debate during the formation of our constitution that revolved around a difference of opinion concerning the wisdom of the general public regarding governance issues. One group believed in a strong central government. The opposing group believed in a stronger state's rights form of government. During this debate it was stated that the wisdom of the great mass of public opinion would not be up to the task of making the critical decisions needed to run the government.

  - I believe one of our founding fathers (perhaps Thomas Jefferson) stated the opinion that *the general public would make good sensible decisions if they were given all of the important facts needed to make informed decisions.* This is critical because it implies that the general public must be told the true facts. If the general public is not told the true facts then by definition they have not been given *the facts*. In addition, after given the true facts, each and every citizen is guaranteed the right to vote — one person, one vote — cast in secret so as to prevent the use of intimidation to force or influence one's vote. Gerrymandering, spinning of facts, voter suppression tactics, etcetera all go against the spirit of honest debate with true facts in the quest for the best solutions for all citizens, not for just a select few.

- The separation of powers was, in my opinion, the most important genius of the founding fathers. Distrust of consolidating all or most of the power of governance in the hands of a select few was consciously a guiding force in structuring the new government of the United States of America. Thus the power of government was divided into the three branches which would need to cooperate with each other, but would be completely independent of each other. Needed cooperation but absolute independence were the essential components for the formation of the three (executive, legislative, and judicial) branches of our government. The strong separation of the power between these three branches has been eroding over the past decades. The motivation behind the erosion is like that motivation behind the gerrymandering and other gaming techniques to manipulate the voting process. That motivation is to win. When individuals' motivations to win escalate to the level of winning at any cost, the individuals' integrity (to tell the truth, to be honest) is not a core concern. When winning at any cost is the major (perhaps the only) goal then the spirit of democratic governance that motivated our founding fathers to write our basic constitution is not relevant to the issue.

- When winning is the ultimate motivation, especially winning at any cost, then the ability to rationalize incorrect behavior greatly increases. Such rationalization permeates our government, our marketplace, our entertainment industry, our religious institutions and so forth. Winning at any cost undermines cooperation. The desire to win at any cost has contributed greatly to the shutdown of our government when the Senate, the House of Representatives and the President cannot cooperate. Vying for the power to win over all opponents undermines any atmosphere of true cooperation.

All of these occurrences are quite understandable, even expected, especially if the system of educating the general public is poor or if educating is supplanted with training.

Banks

When I was growing up in small town USA, banks were considered to occupy a position of importance to the community because banks were that part of the community that helped the individuals of the community to buy cars, houses and get loans for many different requirements. My recollection is that banks prided themselves as being friendly helpers for the local people. One bank in my small town was called Union Trust. Trust was its name as in "You can trust us."

What I remember is that the banks were "community" banks who knew and understood the issues and concerns of the local people. To contrast this sentiment that has all but disappeared, I ask you to consider the words of United States commerce chief, Wilbur Ross who is a self-proclaimed billionaire. He is reportedly one of the richest members of President Trump's cabinet.

On January 24, 2019, *The Guardian* posted at 18.34 EST, "Trump commerce chief wonders why federal workers are using food banks," by Erin Durkin (New York). The following are words from Wilbur Ross on the state of affairs of the 800,000 federal employees who had to go without paychecks for 35 consecutive days because of a partial government shutdown (the longest in the history of the United States of America:

> "I know they are [turning to places like homeless shelters for food donations], and I don't really quite understand why," he said in an interview on CNBC's Squawk Box. "The obligations that they would undertake, say borrowing from a bank or a credit union, are in effect federally guaranteed. So the 30 days of pay that some people will be out, there's no real reason why they shouldn't be able to get a loan against it."

Durkin continues reporting Ross's comments:

> "You're talking about 800,000 workers, and while I feel sorry for the individuals that have hardship cases, 800,000 workers. If they never got their pay – which is not the case, they will eventually get it, but if they never got it, you're talking about a third of a

percent on our GDP. So it's not like it's a gigantic number overall."

Mathematics is not the receptacle of emotions. When humankind, when human individuals, are reduced to numerical entities, they are dehumanized. Can you perceive any humanity in Wilbur Ross's words?

Wilbur Ross's matter-of-factly delivered punch line is an attitude that has been growing for many years. I want to outline the progression to this state of dehumanized understanding of current human reality.

There are three historical events that are like stepping stones to the policy rhetoric voiced by United States commerce chief, Wilbur Ross. In my adult life, the first economic crisis to demonstrate our financial sickness was the Savings and Loan scandal during the 1980s and 1990s. Of the 3,234 savings and loan institutions, 747 failed at the cost of $370 billion dollars of which $341 billion was taken from the taxpayers. Next came the Enron scandal in 2001. Wikipedia reports:

> Enron's shareholders lost $74 billion in the four years before the company's bankruptcy ($40 to $45 billion was attributed to fraud). As Enron had nearly $67 billion that it owed creditors, employees and shareholders received limited, if any, assistance aside from severance from Enron.

The third event prior to Wilbur Ross's insightful revelation of the United States government's level of humanity is the financial meltdown of 2007-08. I do not have hard figures on the vast amount of loss or cost of this horrific economic scandal but I have Wikipedia's assessment of the financial crisis of

2007-08 as: "considered by many economists the worst financial crisis since the Great Depression of the 1930s."

How can the average American citizen come to terms with the huge amount of loss of money attached to this scandal? I offer a small excerpt from *Rolling Stone's* article "The $9 Billion Witness: Meet JPMorgan Chase's Worst Nightmare" written by Matt Taibbi (November 6, 2014, 2:00 PM ET):

> Fleischmann (a tall, thin, quick-witted securities lawyer in her late thirties) is the central witness in one of the biggest cases of white-collar crime in American history, possessing secrets that JPMorgan Chase CEO Jamie Dimon late last year paid $9 billion (not $13 billion as regularly reported – more on that later) to keep the public from hearing.
>
> Back in 2006, as a deal manager at the gigantic bank, Fleischmann first witnessed, then tried to stop, what she describes as "massive criminal securities fraud" in the bank's mortgage operations.
>
> Thanks to a confidentiality agreement, she's kept her mouth shut since then. "My closest family and friends don't know what I've been living with," she says. "Even my brother will only find out for the first time when he sees this interview."
>
> Six years after the crisis that cratered the global economy, it's not exactly news that the country's biggest banks stole on a grand scale. That's why the more important part of Fleischmann's story is in the

pains Chase and the Justice Department took to silence her.

It is my opinion that the financial crisis of 2007-08 was precipitated by greed and perhaps cunning thievery on the part of some of this country's largest banks on a grand scale. Corruption not only permeates our banking (financial system) but also has been and is eating away at our legal system with legal pronouncements like confidentiality agreements. Matt Taibbi continues with further explanations about the coverup:

> She [Fleischmann] was blocked at every turn: by asleep-on-the-job regulators like the Securities and Exchange Commission, by a court system that allowed Chase to use its billions to bury her evidence, and, finally, by officials like outgoing Attorney General Eric Holder, the chief architect of the crazily elaborate government policy of surrender, secrecy and cover-up. "Every time I had a chance to talk, something always got in the way," Fleischmann says.
>
> This past year she watched as Holder's Justice Department struck a series of historic settlement deals with Chase, Citigroup and Bank of America. The root bargain in these deals was cash for secrecy. The banks paid big fines, without trials or even judges – only secret negotiations that typically ended with the public shown nothing but vague, quasi-official papers called "statements of facts," which were conveniently devoid of anything like actual facts.

And now, with Holder about to leave office and his Justice Department reportedly wrapping up its final settlements, the state is effectively putting the finishing touches on what will amount to a sweeping, industrywide effort to bury the facts of a whole generation of Wall Street corruption. "I could be sued into bankruptcy," she says. "I could lose my license to practice law. I could lose everything. But if we don't start speaking up, then this really is all we're going to get: the biggest financial cover-up in history."

Matt Taibbi's article clearly presents to me three telltale signs of a critical, viral and degenerating illness plaguing our country.

1. Confidentiality agreements have become a legal means to keep illegal behavior secret.
2. JPMorgan Chase CEO Jamie Dimon paid $9 billion to keep illegal behavior from public eyes (that would be your eyes and my eyes). It is too obvious that JPMorgan Chase is about making profits and avoiding losses. So, how much did it steal if it had no problem spending $9 billion to keep it hidden away from public view? Answer: A hell of a lot more than $9 billion!!!
3. The original premise for establishing banks was to protect the individual's money from robbers and thieves. Right? Now we have witnessed that the financial system has become the biggest, most successful robbers and thieves of our (the individual citizen's) money that they were supposed to protect.

This one article is very illuminating of the corruption eating away the pillars of our society. I recommend a full reading of Matt Taibbi's article.

Some individuals disagree with the statement that the financial crisis of 2007-08 was the greatest financial crisis since the Great Depression. One individual with whom I spoke believed it to be the second great depression. Public relations just didn't want to label it a depression. Why throw gasoline on a forest fire? However you want to label it, the financial crisis of 2007-08 did not occur or develop in a vacuum. The deregulation during President Bill Clinton's years in office (1993-2001) set the stage for the 2007-08 financial meltdown with the repeal of the Glass-Steagall Act which was an outcome of lessons learned by the devastating Great Depression. There were other individuals who contributed to the forces causing the catastrophe. Angelo Mozilo, CEO of Countrywide Financial, embraced exotic mortgages to borrowers that might not be able to repay the loans. Senate Banking Committee chairman, Phil Gramm worked hard to push through the 1999 repeal of the Glass-Steagall Act. Alan Greenspan, the Federal Reserve chairman, embraced the notion that deregulation was good and that financial institutions could and would regulate themselves responsibly. He was a fan of Ayn Rand, who wrote a novel titled *Atlas Shrugged* that praised the benefits of greed. Greenspan ultimately stated before a congressional committee hearing that he was mistaken about financial institutions regulating themselves responsibly. There were many other individuals whose actions contributed to the progressive infection of corruption within our banking and economic institutions in alliance with corrupting forces within our legal and government institutions.

When I used the Internet to search for the 'financial crisis of 2007–2008' I clicked on Wikipedia's huge article which had a great number of hot links to various key components to attempt to understand how the Great Recession came to be. I will cite a tiny part of this article. You can find it under the "Causes" section.

> The US Financial Crisis Inquiry Commission reported its findings in January 2011. It concluded that:
> ... the crisis was avoidable and was caused by:
> - widespread failures in financial regulation, including the Federal Reserve's failure to stem the tide of toxic mortgages;
> - dramatic breakdowns in corporate governance including too many financial firms acting recklessly and taking on too much risk;
> - an explosive mix of excessive borrowing and risk by households and Wall Street that put the financial system on a collision course with crisis;
> - key policy makers ill prepared for the crisis, lacking a full understanding of the financial system they oversaw;
> - and systemic breaches in accountability and ethics at all levels. — Financial Crisis Inquiry Commission – Press Release – January 27, 2011

In reading some parts of this article while scanning many others, I have come to a conclusion. There were many forces that wanted and still want to shed any blame for the immense tragedy that wrecked the lives of a great many families and individuals. For the sake of brevity, I cite again from the "Causes" section to report some estimate of the financial damage done:

> Falling prices also resulted in homes worth less than the mortgage loan, providing the lender with a financial incentive to enter foreclosure. The ongoing foreclosure epidemic that began in late 2006 in the US and only reduced to historical levels in early 2014 drained significant wealth from consumers, losing up to $4.2 trillion in wealth from home equity. Defaults and losses on other loan types also increased significantly as the crisis expanded from the housing market to other parts of the economy. Total losses are estimated in the trillions of US dollars globally.

Finally, I remember reading some individual in some article commenting that warnings of problems in the financial sector were sounded and recommendations were made after the Saving and Loan scandal of the 1980s and 1990s to avert any more such crisis situations. In that article, the comment was made that these recommendations were not employed. It is my understanding that needed policies, laws, regulation and oversight to rein in the financial sector and Wall Street are still being ignored.

I, as a simple citizen affected by the powers to be, need, and have, a simpler explanation or guide to judge these catastrophes. The resolution of the tension between the exploitive side and the nurturing side within individuals in positions of influence and power were flipped or were consciously turned to the exploiting side of the Decision-

Making Coin. These individuals worked in concert with one another via the common ideology of economic exploitation in a social environment without the necessary laws, policies, regulations and oversight needed to protect the greater community of individuals over the greed of the select few.

Greed is the motivator. Empathy, a requirement for humanity, is deficient or absent altogether. Narcissism is the dominate trait ruling over the human character within the leadership ranks of our critical institutions.

Sex, Food and Humanity

In 1973, Jacob Bronowski copyrighted *The Ascent of Man*. The word, ascent, implies upward movement as in the phrase to ascend the stairs. Whereas ascent implies movement along the vertical axis, progress could be understood as movement along the horizontal axis. In both cases movement is the change from one position to another position. There is, if you will, change relative to some point of origin. Change relative to a point of origin as expressed along the horizontal is easily displayed by the mathematical number line which is commonly known as the X axis:

-(n+1) <-------|-----|-----|-----|----|-----|-----|-----|-----|-------> (n+1)
           -4 -3 -2 -1 0 1 2 3 4

Movement from 0 (the point of origin on the X axis) to the point labeled 4 constitutes a change of 4 units. This is all very elementary and in being so elementary is the best reason to use it to begin my reflections concerning sex, humanity and food. Movement from 0 to -4 is also a movement of 4 units. Mathematicians do not judge 4 to be better or worse than -4 nor is -4 better than or worse than 4. Mathematics is neutral. It is nonjudgmental and merely describes the state of things regarding quantity and position. What is true about the X axis is also true about the Y axis which easily describes the movement from the point of origin in a vertical direction either up or down. It is also elementary that the X axis combined with the Y axis defines two-dimensional space. If we add the Z axis which intersects both the X axis and the Y axis at the point of origin such that it is perpendicular to both, then we have the basic coordinate system that describes three-dimensional space. The number of points along the X axis is immense (infinite to be exact). When we combine the X axis and the Y axis together we have a far greater number. Our biggest, baddest, most awesome super computer cannot name (count) all of the points on the X axis, let alone all of the points on the X axis and the Y axis nor all of the points within the area of two dimensional space. Now grasp the magnitude of three-dimensional space. We are not capable of counting each and every point, but we can locate any one point or selected points if we so desire by using formulas, mathematical conventions and processes to find what we seek. The language of mathematics which has been developing over time allows us to cope with the infinity of infinity.

Language is powerful. The language of mathematics has allowed individuals to wrap an individual in a space suit (more than one individual to be exact), place him or her in a space ship, launch this traveler from Earth to fly to the moon, land, step out and walk or ride on the moon. However, and this is critical, the language of mathematics is neutral. It does not make judgment calls. Minus 4 is the same as plus 4. The only difference is the direction of movement from the point of origin. I want to hammer home the neutrality of the mathematics.

If I want to describe movement from -4 to +4, I can express this movement with the mathematical sentence: $-4 + X = +4$ and then resolve this sentence as follows:

$-4 + X = +4$ [original sentence]
$+4 - 4 + X = +4 + 4$ [Adding 4 to both sides of the equation does not change the equation (basic algebra)]
$0 + X = +8$ $[+4 - 4 = 0; +4 + 4 = +8]$
$X = +8$ [resolution]

In this instance -4 is the point of origin as the starting point of our movement. If we work the movement in the opposite direction we have the following:

$+4 + X = -4$ [original sentence]
$+4 - 4 + X = -4 - 4$ [Subtracting 4 to both sides of the equation does not change the equation (basic algebra)]
$0 + X = -8$ $[+4 - 4 = 0; -4 - 4 = -8]$
$X = -8$ [resolution]

Remember + 8 and - 8 are no better nor worse in magnitude. The plus (+) and the minus (-) only tell the direction of the movement (accurately). One movement is 8 units to the right and the other movement is 8 units to the left. No judgment is made to determine if it is better to move to the left or if it is better to move to the right. It is eight units either way. However, the word 'ascent' in the *Ascent of Man* feels like it implies something inherently beneficial or good in Man ascending to a position higher than his point of origin. In this country, this apparent implication comes not from the language of mathematics. Instead, it comes from our English language. Judgments, the discussions and/or debates concerning issues involving a required judgment are the province of the general language of the culture, society or nation in which the judgments are rendered. The language of mathematics mapped the path and critically facilitated the design of the tools needed to get to the moon from the surface of the Earth. It was the facility of the English language, however, that rendered the judgment that it was beneficial to have such a trip as a goal in the first place even before all of the needed mathematical calculations had been compiled.

The magnitude of reflecting upon sex, humanity and food feels like contending with every point that fills three-dimensional space. Actually, Earth only occupies a very small, perhaps only a minuscule part of the actual area encompassed by three-dimensional space. When I compare my self to Earth as a physical object, Earth is gigantically immense especially when I am standing outside in the middle of a big field, but in truth, Earth is only a tiny speck in our Milky Way galaxy which is only one of many galaxies in the universe. This fact does not mean that humanity by itself does not occupy an infinite amount of points to identify when reflecting upon it.

Consider just one unit of movement along the X axis, the unit of movement from 0 to 1. The point halfway from 0 to 1 is one half (1/2). The halfway point between 0 and one half (1/2) is one quarter (1/4). Between 0 and 1/4 is 1/8. Between 0 and 1/8 is 1/16. Do you see the pattern? There is always a point halfway between any two points. If you work this out to its crazy conclusion, you will discover that there are an infinite number of points between 0 and 1.

To translate this into general English: When considering one element of an array of related elements, that one element will have multiple elements which constitutes its formation. Each of those multiple elements may have elements of their own. Sex, humanity and food are three elements that have multiple elements which constitutes their individual domain and each of those elements within each domain may have elements of their own and so forth and so on just like the movement from 0 to 1 has an infinite set of points. But I do not have to reconcile all of the points between 0 and 1 if I want to get to 4. All I need is to understand that I must travel through 1, 2, and 3 to get to 4 and that all of those units each have the same magnitude (and the magnitude is infinite).

I am not going to discern or even name all of the elements present in sex or humanity or food but I am seeking to travel down a path that has a point of origin and an end point. All reflections come to an end, but I have never had a reflection that exhausted any issue completely. That is a good omen because such a condition reflects the fact that I am still learning and developing, even now as I am moving to my point of exit.

Reproduction is critical to the survival of the species. Human beings are biologically divided into males and females. To reproduce offspring necessary for the species to survive, males and females must both participate in the process of producing more human individuals. This would have been a simple statement 400 years ago. I could have easily written at that time: It takes a man and a woman to make a baby. Now, with the LGBTQ awareness, sexual identity is not so easily defined. More importantly, sexual identity is not the defining quality of the individual. I would have said 'human personality' but I mean something more inclusive than the psychological. Before I tumble into a chaotic discourse, I must admit that I have jumped way ahead of my point of origin. I am more toward the end point when talking about the reality of LGBTQ awareness.

Back to the point of origin. The natural mechanism of the biological reproduction of a human baby is the sperm and the egg. At this point in time, even if fertilization occurs in a test tube, the egg and the sperm are required. The egg is female and the sperm is male. This fact was true in the time of Plato's

Socrates. It was true thousands of years before them. In fact, this is my point of origin.

Our bipedal ancestors living among the animals as mammals had no name for themselves. They had no name for themselves because the voice box had not moved to the spot it now occupies in the biology of our ancestors that began the process of developing a spoken language. The point of origin for this reflection is the time when our primate ancestors lived among the other animals as animals themselves before language, before tools, before fire and villages. At this point of origin, there was no word for male or female. They did not (and this is important) label themselves as males and females. They acted as males and females nonetheless. Our very existence is proof of that observation.

The obviousness of this fact is like the elementary aspect of the number line. The realities that are most obvious to the great majority of individuals serve as excellent points of origin. At this point of origin regarding our reflection of sex, individuals are sexual beings who sexually act but, more than likely, did not give it too much (if any) consideration. The process of reproduction necessary for the continuation of the species simply occurred naturally without fanfare. The critical aspect at our point of origin regarding sexuality is that the desire for sexual activity is hardwired in our biology. Since it is so critical for the continuation of the species, the drive (extreme motivation) to act sexually is extremely strong and is pretty much commanded by the biology as is evident to the great majority of all individuals. Again it is most obvious and apparent once the individual enters puberty. Experiencing puberty is not a choice. Biology takes over. Girls enter their menstrual cycle and boys have wet dreams. Individuals do not choose to be sexual creatures. The biology of the individual forces the issue.

Choice enters into sexuality when the individual is confronted by his or her biology and the actions each individual employs to cope with those biological demands. As we were then, are we still now most like the animals in the wild regarding our sexual behavior? If not, then how do we differ? If we were but have significantly changed, then can we discern what facilitated that change? These are questions that may be best laid aside for the moment until we move a bit further through our reflection, but it is most important to note that we can and have posed these questions.

The point of origin for food is quite simple. We have never not needed to eat. From birth we have needed to consume organic matter (food). As mammals we are first dependent on the organic matter presented to us by our mothers by way of breast milk. From there we begin to demonstrate our tendency to be omnivores. However, did the same distant ancestors which we defined at the point of origin regarding sex start out as herbivores to branch out into being carnivores at times and finally become the omnivores of today? Regardless of what they ate, they had to eat organic matter because mammals are not primary producers on the food chain. They cannot ingest inorganic matter and convert such raw material into the energy-enriched food stuffs needed to carry on our bodily functions. What organic matter was consumed in the earliest years of our ancestors may become more easily discernible as this reflection unfolds itself.

This brings us to the third major element of this reflection, humanity. The point of origin for humanity may be the most illusive. I am not sure that I have, myself, perceived the point where humanity began or begins. Perhaps seeking this point of origin is the driving force behind my reflection? Is the point of origin for humanity when we gained language or when we began making tools or when we began settling in villages or maybe when we painted on cave walls for the first time? Is there a defining element of humanity which could illuminate its point of origin?

In my lifetime I have noted an insult that has been levied toward individuals who have been perceived to have acted badly. The insult is in the form of an observation -- "You are acting like an animal," or " He (or she) acts like an animal." It can also come in the form of an imperative -- "Don't act like an animal." The implication is that our humanity is what separates us from all of the other animals.

If we assert that human beings are in fact significantly different from all other animals of Earth, then the obvious route to take would be to answer the question, "How are we uniquely different from all other animals?" Once this question is answered, an evaluation must be made to ascertain if such differences are significant. The point of origin for the emergence of humanity would be the point where individuals began to act significantly different from all animals. That significant difference would be somehow much more than a sexual or foraging matter. We can cut to the chase by first focusing on how we are different from all other animals. If we can discern no significant differences then we have answered our quest — humanity is not a distinction of significance.

Did our humanity exist before we became enthralled with tool use and tool making? Again, it is too obvious. No other animal species has become tool makers, manufacturers of machines or the builders of concrete jungles. And, yes, this distinction is significant. Is the point of origin for the emergence of early humanity the point where the first individual used the first tool or where he or she manufactured the first tool?

The use of an object as a tool from the surrounding environment is dependent upon the individual discerning the nature of the given object and how that aspect of said object could function as a tool to affect the desired result. This behavior demonstrates that this individual's thinking processes are beginning to move in potentially new directions. Is humanity a cognitive process, a process in which we begin to think differently from all of the other animals?

Hunger, the drive to eat, motivates us to seek out food. The drive to reproduce motivates us to seek out a sexual partner. What drives us to think? Is the process of thinking driven by the need to eat or the need to locate a sexual partner? Hunger and sex are common to all animal species and are driven by strong, very strong biological commands to act accordingly but thinking appears to be something significantly different. Did our mental processes used to acquire food and to alleviate our sexual drive begin to be applied in other pursuits?

Is it perhaps more accurate to understand humanity as being the outcome of the interplay of more than one of the elements that constitutes what we are? Is humanity the interaction of several aspects of biological functions with thinking being part of that array?

During my elementary and high school days, human language was the most distinguishing element of the human animal. However, during my college and adult years certain primates have learned some American Sign Language and have communicated with humans. Dolphin sounds are being studied with the intention to discover if these sounds collectively form a language and if so, then what are the structural components of that language. This presents the question, "Does our language behavior significantly distinguish us form the other animals?" Certainly, our written language and our libraries full of books, especially from texts thousands of years ago, distinguishes us from all other animals. Language, however, especially written language, is about symbol making. Symbol making is about attaching meaning. Symbols represent something that is meaningful.

Enter the cave wall paintings of our ancient ancestors. The one that Jacob Bronowski highlighted (and I believe he did so correctly) was the simple print of a human hand. Perhaps this is the first recorded human signature. Perhaps this is the recorded point of origin for the emergence of humanity. To me this handprint quietly asserts the emergence of consciousness. Consciousness exists when the individual is aware of him or herself as unique in the world and the relationship that exists between the individual and the other living beings in his or her world. Humanity cannot exist without consciousness. Humanity flourishes as the individual reflects upon his or her consciousness.

Consciousness is about awareness. Hunger stimulates the drive to eat and motivates the individual to act. Awareness aids the individual's pursuit to locate and procure the food needed to fend off death by starvation. Hunger moves the individual to hunt. Successful hunting is about the individual's powers of awareness. From the massive amount of diverse visual stimuli presented in the forest to the individual, the hunter must pull out any small movement of the camouflaged prey or the hunter must see and recognize the footprint of the animal being hunted. Tracking an animal requires a large amount of awareness on the part of the hunter reading various signs of the passage and trail left by the prey -- scat, tree rubbings, pawing of the ground and of course the animal tracks. Awareness is not consciousness but consciousness does not exist without awareness. When the hunter becomes aware of and gives meaning to scat found lying on the ground and tree rubbings where a buck has rubbed his antlers or the ground pawing where a doe has urinated to attract bucks and then gives meaning to all of these signs, his consciousness grows.

Reflecting upon the various elements of my awareness stimulates the possibility of perceiving meaningful relationships which, when discovered, increases my consciousness. So, hunger motivates the individual to act (hunt); awareness allows the hunter to gain better experience; reflecting enhances the probability of finding meaning in the experience and, consequentially, consciousness expands. The experienced hunter has a greater consciousness of the animals hunted than the beginner or novice. It is my view that the ancient cave wall paintings are collectively the expression of our early ancestors' consciousness. The handprint however is the point of origin of the individual's consciousness of himself in a very dramatic way.

I searched the internet for "ancient cave wall paintings" to attempt to get some guidance of facts as accepted by my contemporary times. What I found in my hasty, cursory search was information on "The Oldest Cave Paintings in the World." The information was organized from the earliest (6300 BC - 3000 BC) to the oldest (35,600 years ago). This oldest cave is located in Spain and was discovered by Marcelino Sanz de Sautuola. The name of the cave is the Altamira Cave and the information listed ochre and charcoal images of handprints, bison and horses. The incredible quality of these images led to an argument in which some thought the images were too good to be true and therefore might have been fraudulent. In 1902 these images were given the seal of authenticity.

Not being a professional archeologist, I leave the search for ancient artifacts and the ensuing discussions concerning the dating and authenticity of the various finds to the professionals. However, I am a curious individual who is interested in the history of humankind's presence upon Earth.

As such I have availed myself of various publications and texts concerning the subject. In my readings, I have encountered the recording of the phenomenon known as Piltdown Man in the book, *Hen's Teeth and Horse's Toes* by Stephen Jay Gould. Piltdown Man was a paleoanthropological hoax that lasted about 41 years before it was finally declared to be a forgery. I mention this fraud because:

1) I may cite facts that are or will be proven to be inaccurate,
2) humankind's consciousness is still developing,
3) Earth was once thought to be flat, and
4) individuals should always remember that every person regardless of his or her profession or position and regardless of any other element or characteristic is always an entity composed of both light and dark forces in opposing tension affecting every personal decision.

The issue here is not an accurate chronology of archeological history. The issue is the location of the point of origin of the onset of humankind's humanity that distinguishes humankind from all other animals. If the dating of the cave wall paintings in Altamira Cave is correct, then the handprints on those walls are the oldest known record of humankind recognizing its handprint as significantly different from the human figures presented in all other cave wall paintings. What is the significance? It is the individual claiming individuality, claiming uniqueness from the generic representations of humans depicted in the general activities of the times, and it is poetic that the hand was chosen to be highlighted because the opposing thumb is a critical biological distinction from all other animals in the world that has allowed humankind to become massive users of tools and tool makers. I cannot know for sure if the individual who immortalized his or her handprint was aware of the significance of the hand, but it can be easily asserted that the individual knew the difference between his or her handprint and all other representations of "people" in his or her world at the time. Lastly, the "artist" was definitely moved to put his or her handprint on the wall of the cave where other images were considered to be important enough to be recorded. The handprint, his or her handprint, was considered meaningful. The self enters into this individual's consciousness. When the self is recognized as unique and valuable from all other elements in the environment, then humanity begins to emerge.

This being the case, it can be argued that the first burial ceremony would be the depiction of the individual as a unique, meaningful individual worthy of respect and not left to be eaten by scavenger animals. According to another of my hasty, cursory internet searches, Neanderthals intentionally dug graves and buried the dead.

Ker Than wrote, "Neanderthal Burials Confirmed as Ancient Ritual" for *National Geographic* which was published December 16, 2013. In this article he wrote:

> The site at La Chapelle-aux-Saints, France, however, has always been something of a question mark. In 1908, two brothers who were also archeologists uncovered the 50,000-year-old Neanderthal skeleton in the cave, and almost immediately they speculated that the remains were intentionally buried. But a lack of information about the excavation procedures used by the Bouyssonie brothers—as well as the fact that they were Catholic priests—caused many skeptics to wonder if the discovery had been misinterpreted.

In 1999, French researchers reexamined the site. Their excavations, which concluded in 2012, showed that the depression where the skeleton was found was at least partially modified to create a grave.

Wikipedia states that Neanderthals walked on Earth sometime between 400,000 to 40,000 years ago. The El Castillo Cave has the oldest dated handprint at 35,500 BCE.

Humanity is about consciousness. Consciousness is about reflection, specifically about reflections by the individual upon the awarenesses that he or she has gained. Consciousness has the capacity to expand, but capacity is not a predetermination to expand. Expansion is a matter of choice.

Awareness is about collecting details and reflecting. Meaning emerges out of that reflection and the individual becomes conscious of the meaning of related details within his or her awareness. As the individual's consciousness expands, the individual begins to perceive different choices. As decisions are made and related actions are taken, the individual then has the opportunity to reflect upon the outcome(s) of the action(s) taken. In this fashion, consciousness expands. At any level, at any stage in this process the individual can choose to not reflect. The individual can choose to not seek out new details to consider. During this whole process, the individual can act randomly and not choose to consciously look for or seek differences in the environment. Expansion is a choice of action or inaction and which path to take. The expansion of one's humanity, in my understanding, is about the Decision-Making Coin.

The Function of Us

We, the homo sapiens who inhabit Earth, are collectively Nature reflecting upon itself. As Nature reflects upon itself, we have discerned the nature of opposites -- the nature of negative and positive ions of different elements bonding together to form uniquely different and more complex elements which in turn bond with other simple elements or with other complex elements to form yet another unique element of higher complexity and so forth and so on in a process Jacob Bronowski dubbed *"stratified stability."* This process of *stratified stability* over time, change upon change, lead eventually to us, the homo sapiens who collectively form the consciousness of Nature. This consciousness reflects the light and the dark side which constitutes the individual in which human consciousness resides and, therefore, is also an expression of a union of opposites.

Humanity is the result of the resolved tension between the opposites at play within the individual. If humanity is the distinguishing attribute between the human creature and all other animals then there is a measure along a sliding scale that reads on one end "animal-like-behavior" and "distinguishing humankind behavior" on the other side. The direction and magnitude toward one side or the other within the individual is determined by the resolution of the tension between the negative and positive elements; between the dark and the light side, and the choice to flip or not to flip the Decision-Making Coin. To consciously turn the Decision-Making Coin to the Exploiting or the Nurturing side is a significant move toward the humanity side. However, this initial move would be minimized, perhaps even to the point of being insignificant, if the individual chooses to turn to the exploiting side most of the time. Moving away from the randomness of the Decision-Making Coin toward consciously acting is the result of one's awareness, one's reflecting upon that awareness and finding meaning in that reflection thus expanding one's consciousness. Increasing awareness, continuing to reflect and find meaning in that reflection creates a feedback loop that will continue to expand consciousness as this feedback loop continues to hum along.

Each individual in his or her life has control of only those choices within their individual circumstances. Some individuals are in situations that afford them more influence upon the lives of others, and therefore the resolution of the tensions between opposites within those individuals have a greater potential to influence (taint) the coloration of the consciousness of some other individuals. Having the potential to influence is not the same as directly controlling the consciousness of another individual. Ultimately every individual has the absolute control over his or her own choice. However, depending on the circumstances, the given choice of a given individual may be extreme in the consequences of that choice. There have been times that an individual has sacrificed much and has had to endure much because he or she consciously decided to reject the negative or dark side only to endure the animalistic harshness employed by the power of the individual in opposition.

What has been said about the individual is easily transferred to a collective of individuals. The old adage, "birds of the same feather flock together" is a succinct encapsulation of this sentiment. Individuals who gravitate toward one side or the other along this sliding scale tend to reinforce each other and are more comfortable among other individuals of similar persuasions. If the great majority of individuals gravitate toward the randomness of their lives, then the congregation of individuals along the sliding scale of the negative or positive side or the dark side as opposed to the light side is fairly fluid according to the nature of the randomness. As more and more individuals choose to act more consciously in their Decision-Making, then movement of the collective organization toward the dark side or the light side is more stable and less fluid. In this fashion, it can be understood that the nature of the collective consciousness of humankind is akin to the nature of the individual's consciousness.

Humankind understands that, in general, animal behavior is less conscious than human behavior. With this understanding, it is likewise understood that, as the individual moves more toward conscious Decision-Making regarding what action to take, he or she moves away from animalistic behavior and toward the humanity side. This last statement only means that a conscious choice is made. The individual could consciously choose to act animalistically. The individual could consciously choose to exclusively exploit at all times or certainly choose to embrace exploitation as the driving motivation of all decisions made consciously. Such an individual would have consciously chosen to act narcissistically. Such a choice while having some movement toward the humanity side would have a greater magnitude toward the animal side of the sliding scale resulting in a cumulative loss of humanity. This condition is similar to an individual who chooses to nurture as much as is humanly possible but still chooses to be omnivorous. While some movement slides toward the animal side, the magnitude of movement is overall toward the humanity end of the scale.

Just as the soul, or the fate, or the character of the individual is the result of the tension between the opposites within his or her soul or character, so too is the character (or soul) of the collective of individuals the result of affirmed principles formed as the consequence of the tension between shared opposites of the group. Just as unresolved internal tensions and strong opposing forces within an individual causes anxiety and anguish to the point of facilitating the individual to travel down a path of self-destruction, so does unresolved tensions and strong opposing forces between groups of collective individuals within the greater society to feud and war will facilitate the same tendency toward self-destruction of that culture or society.

Is this not the reality in which humankind currently exists? Must it be so? Are we locked in this perpetual struggle until all energy is spent and we submit to self-annihilation? What recourse does the individual (or society) have?

Nature reflecting upon itself is dependent upon the individual. All hope rests with the individual. The hope of the future is that the individual develops into the best human person that he or she can become. To say this another way, the hope of the future is for each individual to achieve the greatest level of humanity that he or she can achieve. Humanity, therefore, resides in the individual and not in the collective. If the collective exudes humanity, it is because of the humanity that radiates from the individuals within the collective. If the collective exudes humanity, it is because of the humanity that radiates from the individuals who occupy positions of influence and/or power within that collective. This is why the single most critical responsibility for any collective of human individuals working together is the facilitation of all individuals to become the best human being above all other animals of the Earth.

This requires a robust educating as opposed to a training of each and every individual. This educating is not about discovering the one area in which the individual demonstrates a natural inclination for remarkable performance and focusing that educating exclusively on that area alone. Emerson warned about such a narrow development during his American Scholar speech on August 31, 1837, which I repeat here for your convenience:

> "Man is not a farmer, or a professor, or an engineer, but he is all. Man is priest, and scholar, and statesman, and producer, and soldier. ... The state of society is one in which the members have suffered amputation from the trunk, and strut about so many walking monsters, -- a good finger, a neck, a stomach, an elbow, but never a man. ... the scholar ... In the right state, he is, *Man Thinking*. In the degenerate state, when the victim of society, he tends to become a mere thinker, or, still worse, the parrot of other men's thinking."

The advent of specialization had advantages and promoted advancements for society; but it, also, created detrimental factors. While specialization facilitated an individual becoming highly skilled in a particular task, it also facilitated individuals ignoring the development of the many, many other necessary tasks required to exercise the responsibility for the maintenance of freedom and independence by yielding all critical decisions to "experts" thereby facilitating the prolonged naïveté of the individual adult. Recall that naïveté is the lack of knowledge whereas ignorance is turning your back on the knowledge that you process.

The hope of the future is the *Individual Thinking* and not the individual who is a well-trained functioning cog in an economic machine or any other narrowly defined entity like lawyer, doctor, scientist, politician or economist etcetera. The hope of the future is not an excellent finger or stomach or elbow or even a brain. The hope of the future is a whole person, fully functioning, developed to his or her highest potential and endowed with all the humanity that distinguishes humans from all of the other animals of Earth.

Over the 25 years of my professional career as an educator I have observed the focus upon high stakes testing of students as a means to evaluate the progress of students which then is used as the determination of the quality of the schools responsible for educating those students. I have come to believe that there are many fallacies in this process of high stakes testing as an assessment tool to measure student progress. A full accounting of the weaknesses that inhabit our current educational system would require at least one full volume of text if not a multivolume collection of texts.

There was an anecdote recorded in the biography of Malcom X about the art of persuasion. Malcom and his teacher were sitting in a diner. Malcom's teacher noticed a glass of water on the counter that had two or three cigarette butts and ashes tinting the water. Obviously this glass of water was used as a makeshift ash tray. Malcom's companion asked the waitress for a glass of water but emphasized that he would like a very clean glass into which his water would be poured. To emphasize his wish he asked the waitress if she could please make sure that the glass was sparkling clean. The waitress affirmed that it would not be a problem. Once the waitress returned with this very clean glass of water, Malcom's teacher reached over and placed the glass of water substituting as an ash tray next to the very clean glass of water and asked, "Now, Malcom, which glass will you drink from?" The obvious response was the very clean glass of water.

To paraphrase, the lesson taught ran something along lines of: "You do not have to disparage the faults of the dirty glass of water. You only have to place a perfectly clean glass of water next to it and the individual will easily choose correctly." This was a lesson that, once encountered, I embraced as extremely sound. While I still have difficulty in always applying it, I seek to follow it as often as possible. At this point, in this reflection, an opportunity to do just that offers itself and I shall attempt to comply with my best effort.

Contemporary educators have a choice to make. The age-old Intelligence Quotient (I.Q.) has a competing theory describing human intelligence. With Dr. Howard Gardner's theory of multiple intelligences (M.I.) which he developed around 1983, a new approach to educating the individual emerged. I first became aware of Dr. Gardner, a professor of education at Harvard University, by reading his *Frames of Mind: The Theory of Multiple Intelligences*. I read two other titles of his and from there forward attempted to integrate my understanding of M.I. into my educating practices.

I.Q. is a single measure of an individual's intelligence which does not render as much information about a student (other than rating a given student's intellectual prowess according to his standing within the group of his or her peers). M.I. rates each individual based on several unique intelligences. At first Gardner identified the following seven:

1. linguistic
2. logical-mathematical
3. musical
4. spatial
5. body-kinesthetic
6. interpersonal (intelligence about others), and
7. intra-personal (intelligence about one's self).

Each intelligence had to have a unique neural pathway in order to be considered an intelligence. This was the compelling criterion that motivated me to accept Gardner's assertions that each was a unique intelligence. Number 8, naturalistic intelligence (the classification and understanding of nature), was added later to the list. Before I retired from teaching, a ninth intelligence, existential intelligence (the intelligence to wrestle with the questions of why we live and why we die, etcetera), was being considered and evaluated. At the time of my reading about existential intelligence, Dr. Gardner had not determined if this was in fact a separate intelligence. I recall that he had not discerned a unique pathway for this ninth intelligence. Not being bound to prove my position, I fully embraced existential intelligence as a bona fide ninth intelligence without his stamp of approval.

Having been an experienced middle school classroom teacher for many years before I read Dr. Gardner's texts, I had read about middle school students demonstrating the ability to excel at mathematics while struggling with language arts. Other middle school students demonstrated the opposite tendency where they excelled in language arts but struggled with mathematics. The frequency of my experiencing this phenomenon allowed me to relate to and embrace Howard Gardner's findings.

The Critical Skills Institute presented to me through Antioch/New England Graduate School and M.I. presented to me via Dr. Howard Gardner as well as other educating issues like educating over training constitute the very clean glass acquired to be placed alongside another glass containing I.Q. scores, high stakes testing, training and narrowly defined areas of learning (the four core curriculum areas of English, math, science and history), compared to the 12 areas of focus defined by the Critical Skills Institute. I choose to drink from the former, very clean, glass.

No doubt, as I am still breathing and my mind is still functioning, my reflecting behavior has not come to an end. However, it is time for me to bring this session to a close.

To Summarize What I Have Learned (Correctly or Incorrectly)

I have learned that Western civilization was formed upon an incorrect philosophical premise which it continues to embrace and reinforce. There is no pure disembodied "good" or pure disembodied "evil". The human character is the fusion of opposites, the positive and the negative. Any harm or help originates from within the human individual. Individuals can act collectively for positive outcomes or individuals can act collectively for negative outcomes. The nature of the universe is more like the yin-yang, the union of the positive and the negative. The nature of the universe is about the resolution of the tension between opposites. This is not to say that I believe every descriptive assertion ascribed to the yin-yang as being accurate. That world view in its completeness is from a culture that is not my culture and in which I have not matured. My culture however has plenty of evidence to support the nature of the universe as the union of opposites, the union of the positives and the negatives.

I, like every other human individual, have been born into a dynamic universe already churning with the resolutions of prior tensions between opposites. Just like every other adult human individual, I am the consequences of the past. I am the consequences of my mother's upbringing and the experiences of her life before my birth as I am also the consequences of my father's upbringing and the experiences of his life before I was born. I am the consequences of the tension between my mother's resolutions of her life and my father's resolutions of his life. I am also the consequences of the tensions between the positive and negative forces within the predator-priest who deceived, manipulated and betrayed me when I was 15. In this light, I am not unlike a great many other individuals in my generation or the generations who came before me.

My birth and my early upbringing are the consequences of that cumulative past. I am the consequence of all of these interacting forces until I begin to take possession of my own life. At the point of possessing myself, I become the foundation of the future. To be a healthy, nurturing, beneficial foundation, *I must not seek to pass on the negative consequences of the past.* This is done by minimizing the activity of my negative side and enhancing the activity of my positive side. Additionally, I must recognize that I do have a negative side and that it is my responsibility to contend with that side of my self that is negative. Each of us, even those of us whose actions are perceived mostly as extremely positive, has a negative side as well as a positive side that forms the whole of the human character.

It is critical to understand that the resolution of the tension between opposites is not always positive. It can be negative as well or even neutral (do nothing, deny, suppress and bury it deep). Resolution of tension means only that a decision concerning what to believe, what to say, or how to act, etcetera, has been made to traverse that acceptable path. That path could be positive or negative; nurturing or exploiting; animalistic or humanistic. That said, I return to my tabled observation made on page 5: "So much for my sacred oaths" which was a reference to my divorce (the breaking of marital vows) and my pledge to never marry again. We are born naïve and as we grow up we diminish our naiveté. However, as we grow we experience new environments and situations which can place us in a state of new naiveté. Vows and pledges made in a state of naiveté should not be adhered to if health and welfare become compromised to the point of becoming self destructive and continues to grow in its destructiveness. The nature of being naïve is to be highly susceptible to making errors. Sometimes these errors can be quite harmful. Once the error is recognized as significant, then to stay welded to that error is the demonstration of ignorance. Such errors should be rectified. If the rectification means accepting that the vow or pledge was honestly made but made from a naïve understanding, then that vow or pledge should be considered null and void.

While I learned this lesson through the experience of having to end one marriage and then marrying a second time, there are other situations which demonstrate this understanding. The case of an individual signing a confidentiality agreement is also noteworthy. Companies which have employees sign confidentiality agreements so that the companies' unethical and illegal activities cannot be made public is a vow, pledge or "agreement" that under such circumstances should be rectified. Confidentiality agreements should be terminated if it can be shown that such agreements hide harmful, exploitive, unethical or illegal action or behavior or intent to carry out such action. There should be a mechanization (like legal divorces) that allows an individual to treat such confidentially agreements as null and void. Additionally, regarding confidentiality agreements, there should be laws prohibiting such abusive confidentiality agreements being required in the first place. Individuals caught in such confidentiality agreements should be able to blow the whistle with impunity and public support.

It was unavoidable for me to come face to face with my negative side when attempting to heal from the trauma I experienced from my encounter with my predator-priest confessor. The vast dark ocean of rage and anger stimulated by the terror and hate activated within the negative side of my self had to be seen and felt and reckoned. Having no real, accessible target upon which to spew my poisonous venom, I turned my desire to destroy upon myself. My light, the positive of me, came face to face with the negative, the dark of me, on a late afternoon when I was 15 alone in the middle of an empty school playground. Somehow I found that there was enough value in me, a bright spark, worth defending such that I would not cooperate in snuffing it out. I would not allow others to snuff it out even if they were more powerful than myself and might be able to take the life from my body. I would kick and scratch, punch and do whatever I could to fight to keep my light lit for as long as possible. However, I have learned that healing from such trauma involves much more than surviving, but I would not heal if I did not survive. I walked off of that playground alone, angry, defiant, willful and damaged.

At 68 I am not the same as that boy of 15. I have healed a great deal even though I am not completely healed. I may never be fully healed but I am greatly relieved and the great ocean of rage, anger and hate has been transformed into an immense pool of sadness. Notice that sadness is still the opposite of joy; but, the dark side of me is less pitch black and horrifying. The positive side of me is much stronger and more than adequately supports the ability to feel the sadness without harm. If I have succeeded in my journey through the challenges of my life's travels thus far, it is because of the development of my consciousness.

Along the way I have been fortunate enough to have met individuals who, unlike the predator-priest, had well developed positive sides and nurtured me forward toward a brighter affect. What I developed, probably as an outcome of my predator-priest encounter was an over-active awareness of my environment and all that was in it. This hyper vigilance is a possible outcome due to experiencing severe trauma.

My mother may have also contributed to my hyper vigilance because I never knew when the positive, nurturing side of her would disappear and I had to face the negative, dark side of her. As an example, when I was doing my assigned duty to wipe the dinner dishes, she struck me along the side of the face with the wet rag. It stung. I flinched. To this day I have no idea why I was hit. It was important to know which way the wind was blowing concerning my mother because if I did not see the warning signs, I would have to pay the price for my lack of awareness. The irony of this situation, however, is that I discovered in treatment that my mother's behavior (her aggressive, authoritarian side) taught me to not defend myself. Hence I was even more easily preyed upon by the predator-priest.

Hyper vigilance is about self-protection. While hyper vigilance is very helpful in providing protection, there are aspects of it that are very annoying. Being on a constant alert for danger requires some adjustments, one of which is hiding your constant vigilance. The silver lining to this newly incorporated life strategy is the development of a very active sense of awareness which facilitates the perception of the wondrous as well as the dangerous. This duality of discerning the wondrous and the dangerous over the years is the beating heart that so fully embraces the mantra embossed on Joe's Honor Coin. For me to survive the trauma of the consequences of my cumulative past, I had to see a thing for what it is (was); nothing more, nothing less. With the needed awareness to achieve this prescript, I also discovered the wondrous nature of existence. Thus is my joyful embracing of the advice to remember that wonder and mystery are forever and always present. When reflecting upon both sides of Joe's Honor Coin, the intricacies of The Decision-Making Coin become easily understandable, commendable and worth abiding as is the case for Two Sides of the Same Coin. These three coins form for me a gestalt complete in itself and robust enough to serve as an excellent value system to assist my learning and Decision-Making. The fact that the value system encompassed by the three coins is free from allegiance to any particular tradition worshiping any deity or collection of deities is a significant benefit. Christians of the various forms of Christianity, Buddhists, Hindus, Protestants, Agnostics and Atheists, etcetera, could easily ascribe to this value system without betraying their practice of what they consider as sacred.

The value system and world view encompassed by these three coins is definitely secular. Reward or punishment for behavior is the natural outcome of that behavior. The given behavior which exploits or nurtures, destroys or creates, competes or cooperates and so on and so forth has natural consequences that over time may inform the individual regarding what may be gained and what is lost.

However, what should the response be when one encounters an individual or individuals who seek only to exploit others? What is to be done? The resolution of the tension between the positive and the negative within the individual and within the collective is pretty much the same answer. Naïveté and ignorance are the major forces with which to contend. Educating each and every individual to their highest level is a requirement, not a luxury. Educating over training is the primary goal with training being a basic step toward facilitating a more robust development of the higher levels of educating the individual to facilitate a more expansive consciousness leading to an expanding humanity within each individual within the community.

Educating, increasing awareness, continual reflection leading to an increasing and penetrating consciousness will hopefully lead to an expanding humanity practiced throughout the collective of individuals. In my experience, this point of view has been refuted as naive, simple minded, pie in the sky Utopianism, impossible to achieve, childish (like believing in Santa Clause and the Easter Bunny), and so forth and so on. I am to this day still amazed and astonished at these refutations.

It is only a matter of will. It is only a matter of the will to choose (to counter acting randomly). It is only a matter of the will to choose to nurture over the will to exploit. If the vast majority of individuals choose exploiting others over nurturing others, then that community will experience the results of that choice. (This might be our current condition.) If it is otherwise and nurturing is chosen over exploiting, then the experienced outcome will be different. It really is that simple.

The great difficulty is the developing, maintaining and expanding one's self-discipline to exert the will to develop, maintain and expand the light, nurturing side of the self when the dark, negative side is stimulated and seeks to override the nurturing side of the self. However, self-defense is a requirement of Nature. This is where the evolution of community and social institutions becomes important. Quite possibly, self-defense against exploitive behavior and harm might have been the impetus for moving toward and developing community and the various social institutions. It must be remembered as it has been demonstrated, as it may always be demonstrated, that no matter what the advancement is, it will have a negative side as well as a positive side. As such social institutions degrade toward the negative and as those individuals, themselves, who occupy positions of influence and power degrade from their positive, nurturing side to their negative, exploiting side, so will all advancements morph to reflect the consequences of that movement. As the various social institutions become corrupted toward the exploitive side while abandoning their nurturing mandate, that given society, that community, becomes unhealthy. If the trend is left unabated the society will die.

Educating (over training) every individual to the highest level possible is preventative care. Even with the best preventative care, some individuals may, through ignorance, choose exclusively (or with high frequency) to exploit, thereby becoming more and more narcissistic. These individuals will inflict fear and sadness in the lives of those they encounter. I know through experience that such a situation will result in the extreme with rage, anger, vengeance and a very strong desire for retribution, etcetera. Mini wars or great wars will ensue. Wars, skirmishes, fights and altercations are social illness. If unhealed, death and perhaps annihilation ensue. Narcissistic behavior in breeding anger and fear triggers self-defense at some point and confrontation (war) abounds.

Tragically, I perceive that it is not common knowledge that peace (harmony) can never be achieved through confrontation, nor competition. War is physical competition in the extreme. Harmony and peace is the only solution. Anything less is more about suppression that will most likely fester at some level until it bursts forth like an infection poised to bring the body politic to its knees, perhaps even to its deathbed. Just as the individual must on a daily basis struggle and hopefully be successful in keeping his or her dark side in check, so, too, must the society at large keep its dark side in check. The function of our institutions is to promote the positives and retard the negatives. Natural consequences will alert us to our progress in this matter like pain alerts us to some body malfunction. The greater the malfunction, the greater the pain.

When I was in therapy I was encouraged to be focused on four emotions -- glad, sad, mad or scared. These same four can be expressed as happiness, sadness, anger or fear. While my facility with the English language affords me a larger vocabulary to describe my emotional state, avoidance behavior and over intellectualization can impede healing. I had to be watchful that *the brilliance in my ignorance* did not erode or block my healing. Focusing on these four basic emotional states gives clarity to an individual's underlying, basic emotional condition. Focusing on these four helped immensely, especially when reflecting upon the effects of the trauma of my life. Reflecting to discern the emotional state influencing actions taken is very helpful for bringing awareness of hidden motivations.

What I have learned about me and the effects of trauma upon me is that anger covers sadness. The intensity of the anger is fueled by the intensity of the deep sadness. Mad feels incredibly powerful. When you are terrorized (scared out of your wits) you become paralyzed (literally) like a deer frozen in the headlights of an oncoming speeding truck. Being frightened into immobilization may reduce the individual to uncontrollable weeping. I do not believe this weeping originates from sadness. This uncontrollable weeping is from fear.

During a few treatment sessions, I experienced uncontrollable weeping bouts. In that state during those times I consciously felt absolute vulnerability. Anyone could have done anything they wanted to do to me. In that state, I was absolutely defenseless and I was 60 years old and physically well. Sexual abuse is not about physical harm, although physical abuse can coincide with the sexual abuse. The long lasting and deeply devastating harm from sexual abuse is psychological and emotional trauma to the human spirit.

Intense vulnerability without the presence of trust engulfs the individual with intense fear expanding into terror. I was not cognizant of any of these insights at the time of my actual experience with the predator-priest. Understanding came as a gradual process through many treatment sessions.

Once again in a place of relative safety and free from the presence of the predator-priest, I felt **MAD**. I was angry about being betrayed, angry about my role in being betrayed, angry that I was deeply frightened, angry that there was no one to protect me, angry that I needed to be protected, angry that the police would not be called, angry that I would not be believed, angry that I had no power... I... was... angry. I would later learn that I was angry even when I smiled. [If you substitute the word "hurt" for "angry" and reread this paragraph you will see what I later learned in treatment and what the issue was that provoked the second year and a half of treatment.] So mad, sad and scared are emotions of which I am well acquainted. Feeling glad, feeling really happy was a challenge.

Somewhere along the way of my travels, I encountered an anecdote attributed to Albert Einstein. It was reported that Einstein believed that an individual would be extremely fortunate if he or she engaged in pursuing the solution to an acceptable quest which would take a lifetime to complete. I was struck by the good sense of that aspiration — to find an enriching goal that would require one's life to achieve. The quest I deemed as consistent with Einstein's notion was for me to discover what it means to be a human male and to achieve the best representation of such.

I am a male with a spirit composed of opposites, composed of a vast and diverse array of positives and negatives, such as the capacity to nurture or the capacity to exploit. I have the capacity for rage and the capacity for calm resolve. I was born and have lived among individuals who are the consequences of the resolution of the tension of their past light and dark forces and I became the foundation of the future at the point of possessing my self. I have discovered and embraced a value system robust enough to guide my decisions and actions. This value system is encompassed by three coins which serve to remind and to focus my attention as well as to be an outward expression to others who wish to understand the bases of my life's aspirations. I struggle with the tension between the positive and negative forces within me as I struggle to cope with the negative outcomes of the actions of others who also struggle with the same internal tension. I struggle with the negative outcomes of those individuals who are unaware of these issues, who ignore these issues or who consciously choose to exploit as often as possible.

Sometime between 1968 and 1970, I recorded the following in the little black book which was my journal. It is lost now, so I am unsure of exactly when I wrote the following:

> The purpose of one's life
> Is to find the reason for one's death.

Somehow this insight felt to be intimately interwoven in the understanding of what it would mean for me to be the fully developed representation of a human male. Learning seems to be at the heart of this stated purpose. The answer is in the understanding of the four emotions: glad mad, scared and sad as well as the understanding of the tension of opposites.

Fear, being scared, invokes self-defense. As fear increases to the level of terror, rage is the solution for overcoming fear. Rage is powerful or at least feels powerful to the extent that feeling enraged overcomes feeling scared. This is true in the moment of conflict in which one must defend oneself. After the heat of battle, away from harm, feelings subside, anger sets in, revenge or retribution (an eye for an eye) simmers and schemes. At this stage, the individual's reflections are not upon any sadness with the exception of feeling the sadness for what was most precious and lost in the conflict. This sadness lasts until it translates into more anger. It is my belief that this added anger attains at least the same level of the experienced sadness if not higher. The combatant stays in that state until retribution is imposed. Fear invokes self-defense which stimulates destructive tendencies. Fear stimulates the negatives.

If the individual's life is not threatened, then fear is not experienced. Anger in the world is reduced to a minimum when fear is removed from the environment. Fear is removed in the world when a state of harmony exists. Harmony is not slavery. Slaves do not live or feel harmony. Slaves live in bondage under fear of reprisal at the whim of the will of the owner. Harmony is the state of cooperation between free individuals for mutual benefit.

Sadness is about loss. Sad does not feel like glad. Glad is about gain. Sad is the opposite of glad. Fear is the opposite of security. Fear is associated with danger. Security is associated with safety. So sad and fear are on the negative side while glad and safety are on the positive side. Sadness can evoke anger in the same way that fear can. Fear is at least an uncomfortable feeling and anger helps alleviate that uncomfortable feeling. Sadness can also become an uncomfortable feeling and individuals, myself included, have covered over their sadness with anger. Unlike fear, sadness is not removed by harmonious living between mutually cooperative free individuals. Death of loved ones will occur. Losses will happen even if harmonious living is the state of the collective of individuals. Losses will occur as individuals learn at their individual learning rates. Mistakes will happen. Goals will be postponed. "Feelings" will be accidentally hurt especially when learning how to live through your naïve understandings.

Harmony, however, is the solution for sadness. It is the harmony within the individual, as opposed to the harmony within the community, that alleviates the individual's sadness. The harmony within the community is extremely affective and effective in assisting the individual's internal search for his or her needed harmonious process of becoming educated. Harmony is the result of educating the individual. The educating process as it progresses develops the increasing potential for the individual to discover how to internally harmonize through his or her reflections. When experienced, sadness can be felt, absorbed and internalized without fear or harm. Sadness will be understood as an acceptable outcome of the great joy (gladness) received through the encounter that has now ended. The educating process as it progresses should reveal that there is much joy possible in a world of harmonious living.

So, of the four emotions: mad, sad, scared and glad, three are attributed to the negative side with glad being the only one attributed to the positive side. Gladness (joy) not needing to be alleviated, is experience unassisted. Mad, sad and scared are alleviated through harmony. The reason for my death was revealed to me as my educating developed my consciousness to the level at which I begin to feel the harmony of the universe. The elements that have joined together to make the uniqueness that is me are to be recycled and not wasted. I am here for my visit and as exciting and challenging, as wonderful and as heart wrenching it has been at times, it must come to an end. It is my hope that I feel the sadness of leaving Earth, grateful that I had the experience, and that I feel the least amount of fear of the unknown as I possibly can. The purpose of my death is to die well. The purpose of my life is to have learned how to do so.

About the Author

My official retirement was June 2004. I began my career as a professional educator in September 1979, but I was paid to teach swimming lessons to non-swimmers and to train lifeguards when I was 15. That is a combined 38 years of being formally engaged with students needing to learn what I was hired to teach. During those years I have attended my share of workshops, training sessions, conferences, college classes in various Educational Departments and numerous faculty meetings and parent conferences. As a professional educator, I have worked in the public sector and the private sector. I have been a regular classroom teacher, a special education resource room teacher, a curriculum developer, a principal and a director of educational services for adolescents housed in a psychiatric hospital. Along the way I have developed some strong views on the many aspects of education. Having taught in many different work environments, I needed to develop the skill of meeting the requirements of each different situation while staying true to my beliefs about the responsibility, ethics and inherent obligations of adults nurturing students.

I have been divorced. I am in my second marriage. My first marriage produced twin sons who are in their thirties. The relationship with my current wife is 24 years and still going strong. I am now a Type II diabetic and I have been diagnosed with a rare blood disorder that cannot be cured.

My mother was a devout Roman Catholic and steadfastly raised her family to be devout Catholics. The whole family attended Mass every Sunday. My dad underwent the procedure to convert to the Roman Catholic Church and be baptized in my mother's faith. Such was the power of The Church in my mother's life. At age 15, I was targeted by a predator-priest who was my confessor. I am an adult survivor of child sexual abuse.

www.ingramcontent.com/pod-product-compliance
Lightning Source LLC
LaVergne TN
LVHW011420080426
835512LV00005B/168